7 RULES TO BECOME EXCEPTIONAL AT CYBER SECURITY

A practical, real-world perspective for cyber security leaders and professionals

Chirag D Joshi

ISBN-13: 978-0-6486623-8-9

A special thanks to my wife Urvi for her encouragement that made this book possible.
I also express my deep gratitude to Trish Naidoo, Sameer Karamchandani, and Rahul Sapre for their support.

I dedicate this book to my family and its newest additions, my furry best friend Leo, and my nephew Rudra.

Table of Contents

Introduction

The word exceptional means something out of the ordinary. It implies something outstanding and remarkable. Something that is unusual. This book is about exceptional – exceptional professionals for an exceptional time in an exceptional field.

We live in exceptional times, in a world amazingly interconnected by the internet and technology. A world where we can reach more people than ever before in human history through devices that can fit in the palm of our hands. A world where every minute every day on the internet, consumers spend over a million dollars on goods and services, hundreds of thousands of hours of content is streamed, millions of messages and emails are exchanged, and hundreds of thousands of people are actively using video conferencing applications. This happens every minute, every day!

In this exceptional world, the ability for people to trust the technology to do its job while keeping them safe and secure is at the heart of making it all work. This is where cyber security comes in, to enable human progress through trust in technology. A truly exceptional endeavour. This, along with other factors laid out in this book, have necessitated a rapid and commensurate change in the role of cyber security leaders and professionals. A need for them to be exceptional because the importance of these individuals to their organisations, communities, and countries has never been greater. The availability of skilled cyber security resources is one of the more pressing challenges faced by organisational globally, further highlighting the need for well-rounded cyber professionals.

Fortunately, the interest in cyber security across the world has never been greater. This includes but isn't limited to corporate boardrooms, documentaries on major entertainment streaming services, newspaper headlines, geo-political issues, election debates, and government advisories. Cyber security is now a multi-billion-dollar market and is only expected to keep getting bigger at a rapid pace globally.

The swift rise in the importance of cyber security is driven largely because reliance on technology keeps increasing exponentially. Technology has helped improve the quality of life and transformed communication, entertainment, education, shopping, healthcare, collaboration, commerce, and a host of other areas. It has also helped bring transparency and visibility to social issues like never before.

Now, cyber security relates to protecting information, systems, and devices, and by extension, people and organisations that rely on them. As technology evolves, so do the cyber threats since cybercrime is a very profitable endeavour with relatively lower risk than other forms of crime for the most part. Attribution and prosecution of cybercrime is still very difficult and the barrier to entry is very low. In this new world, cyber security is also vital to national security and prosperity and consequently a very important avenue for nation-state adversaries to gain the upper hand in conflicts, cause disruptions, obtain diplomatic leverage and seek shortcuts to economic prosperity.

Sadly, cyber security incidents, scams, and breaches are not new. However, we are witnessing a massive surge in their occurrence and sophistication. The global cost of cybercrime is expected to be in the trillions of dollars very soon. Cyber Security incidents have caused impacts beyond business losses and data breaches.

We've seen a direct impact on human lives and the economic health of nations through attacks like Ransomware. Especially noteworthy instances of these were the Colonial Gas Pipeline incident in the United States which affected millions of people, and incidents that have impacted hospitals and healthcare entities who couldn't provide needed care to their patients. In fact, in 2022, the country of Costa Rica had to declare a national emergency due to devastating ransomware attacks! The scourge of cybercrime hits organisations of all sizes, but consequences for small businesses who can't afford or are unaware of good cyber practices are far more pronounced. A lot of these go out of business shortly after suffering a significant cyber incident.

In response to these challenges, we're starting to see significant investments in cyber security by governments and businesses. However, benefits realisation and value delivery from these investments leave a lot to be desired. Senior executives and boards are still unsure of their organisation's true cyber security exposure and posture. There is also a lack of clarity on what an appropriate target state and proportionate spend would look like. On the other hand, cyber security professionals are faced with ever-increasing workloads and multiple competing priorities. They struggle to get the requisite support and resources from their business leaders. These challenges highlight the need for cyber security leaders and professionals to evolve and operate in a different, more business-aligned, and engaging manner. While there are plenty of thick technical textbooks, research papers, courses and certifications, there needs to be more in the way of some good old-fashioned succinct, practical, and actionable guidance that helps cyber security professionals deliver massive value to their organisations and in the process excel in their own careers. A guide that helps senior executives and business leaders understand what good looks like from a cyber security perspective and accordingly support and enable their teams. Hence, I decided to write this book and present seven rules focused on exactly these outcomes – bridging the gap between business and cyber security, maximising value from cyber security, enabling organisations in pursuit of their strategic goals, and helping professionals become truly exceptional. These rules are articulated in an engaging, conversational style with a focus on real-world outcomes. In my view, no exceptional leader or professional can maximise their potential without the right differentiating skills and an authentic brand to complement their technical knowledge, so the book takes these attributes into account.

Now, my experience includes building, leading, and implementing cyber security, risk, compliance, and awareness programs in multiple countries across various industries. These industries include but aren't limited to financial services, energy, healthcare, and universities. I have held senior positions, including executive leadership in large, complex organisations, and led teams and cyber transformation initiatives with multi-million-dollar budgets. My previous book – "7 Rules to Influence Behaviour and Win at Cyber Security Awareness" was a huge success and has been purchased in over 11 countries across the world. I have delivered cyber security keynotes and presentations at numerous conferences and international forums, and have won awards and recognitions in organisations I have worked in. I am privileged to have been a Board Director for ISACA Sydney and continue to be one at the time of writing this book. Additionally, I run my own podcast on cyber security that has accomplished professionals join me in sharing their insights.

While I have achieved success, I am still far from hitting my potential, so I continue to strive and improve each day. However, I am sharing my story so you know that the information in this book is coming from someone credible. Someone who has done the hard yards, learnt valuable lessons both from wins and failures and can provide insights on what works in the real world. From a personal standpoint, I have lived an immigrant experience in multiple countries and have achieved success accounting for all the positives and challenges this journey comes with.

Following the rules in this book has allowed me to achieve continued career success. I have also seen other professionals accomplish great things by exhibiting these practices. I am confident these rules will help you become a more effective and successful professional and leader. Even exceptional.

If you have read my previous book, followed my podcast or my social media channels, you know I am not a fan of overcomplicating concepts. Simplicity is the essence of effective communication. This book has been kept short and to the point by design. Far too often, people have to go through voluminous texts to find a couple of useful takeaways. My goal for this book is to provide you with valuable nuggets of information without suffering through long-winded theories. I hope that you can finish reading this book in a few hours and come back to it repeatedly as needed. I have included several links in the resources section where you can do more detailed reading in your interest areas. While the lessons of the book are simple, that doesn't mean they are easy. It will take persistence and a desire to grow and succeed on your side to make the takeaways and insights work for you. But by picking up this book, I can tell you have these qualities, and I commend you for it. With that, let's get started!

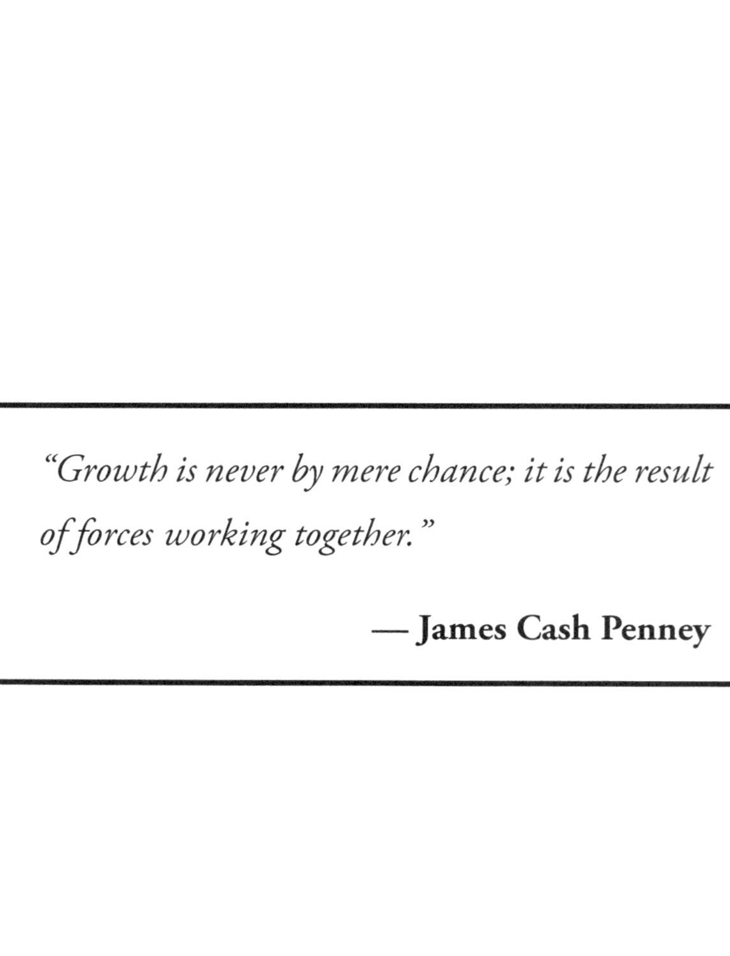

"Growth is never by mere chance; it is the result of forces working together."

— James Cash Penney

Develop a Business-aligned Mindset

Mindset is the foundation on which continued excellence is built. For cyber security to deliver value, cyber security leaders and professionals need to develop a business-aligned mindset. This involves having a good understanding of your organisation's business as well as the industry landscape you operate it. Developing a business-aligned mindset allows a cyber security function to truly play an enabling role in their organisation's success. This is essentially the reason for its existence; if an organisation goes out of business, then there is no cyber security function left. On the face of it, this should be obvious. However, in the midst of daily operational grind and with the pressures of running a security function in a fast-changing threat environment, this can be lost sometimes.

So, let's be clear, regardless of the role you occupy or wish to occupy – be it a Chief Information Security Officer, cyber security engineer, architect, analyst, or awareness manager, a business-aligned mindset is paramount to becoming exceptional.

Some of the critical steps you need to take to build this mindset start with developing a really good knowledge of the products and services that bring in the revenue to your organisation. You should understand the structure of the business functions and the key people in them. Get visibility of the big-ticket programs and projects in these areas. Understand the benefits that these programs intend to deliver. By programs, I don't mean just the technology-related ones. I mean those that allow the lines of business to meet their revenue targets or strategic commitments. Not all programs or projects with significant cyber security implications are technology-led. This same business-aligned thinking applies to government organisations as well, where the focus should be on key services expected by the citizens and community.

Now, the simplest and most obvious way to develop business understanding is by actually talking to business stakeholders. However, in my experience, security professionals spend way too much time talking to technology folks and not nearly enough time talking to people in lines of businesses. I hope by picking up this book, you'll endeavour to get that balance right. Below are some resources you can leverage to understand and help your business:

- Company strategy and performance updates

- Products and services listings on corporate websites

- Key market updates and quarterly financial reports

- Organisational mission, vision, purpose, and values

- Company intranet and enterprise social networking channels.

- Senior Executive updates and documentation on business and technology strategies

- Reviewing major initiatives for business and technology teams planned for the year

- Attending or reading salient points from the Annual General Meetings

- Organisational charts that explain structures in the business lines

- Regulations that apply to your industry especially related to cyber security

- Knowledge of key competitors, their offerings and notable media releases made by them

- Awareness of major news and updates including geo-political or international issues that could have an impact on your industry

Getting a good handle on these will put you in a strong position to assess if your current cyber security processes, skills, and engagement models are setting the organisation up for success. You will be able to contextualise your understanding of cyber security threats and controls with what truly matters to organisation. It will help you connect your work with the strategies that are material to your organisation's survival and growth. This is vital to delivering value. You win when your business wins. It is just that simple.

Another key part of building a business-aligned mindset is getting a good handle on finances. We live on an economic planet. Simply put - Money matters. It matters to organisations of every shape and size. It matters to commercial enterprises, government organisations, and Not for Profits as well. Not for Profits are also Not for Loss. So, if finances are important to organisations and cyber security is about enabling organisations – cyber security leaders need to be adequate in the basics of financial management and budgeting. Now, note I used the word – adequate. You don't need to be a finance expert. My recommendation is that you build good relationships and cadence with the finance and procurement teams in your organisation. As each organisation is different, how they prefer to manage finances, fund, and source activities may vary. Working with finance and procurement teams will help you understand the organisational dynamics related to these activities. This will enable you to formulate the right funding mechanism and go-to-market strategies for various initiatives.

Another benefit of building relationship with these teams is that it gives you insights into potential gaps in the procurement process that could allow purchase of systems or services without the necessary security due diligence. This could make the organisation vulnerable to cyber threats as a result of weak vendor security practices. We will look at vendor cyber risk management in more detail in Rule 2.

Now, understanding finances and demonstrating to the business that you can be trusted with them enable you to move up in the organisation and become very effective in your role. This includes everything from being able to frame business cases, understand and articulate proposals, set, and manage team budgets.

Even for cyber security professionals in very technical roles or those with no direct reports, having a foundational knowledge of organisational finance mechanics helps them present their requests for funding, resourcing, or support for initiatives in a more informed manner. They immediately become more valuable to their leaders since they understand the check and challenge that their leaders face from more senior executives and can accordingly help frame the message.

An important thing to understand in finance is change and run costs. Simply put, run costs are your ongoing costs, while change costs are your one-time costs. For e.g., if a program is introducing a Privileged Access Management (PAM) solution in the organisation to address insider threats and bolster access controls, the initial uplift cost to introduce the tool in your environment could be a change cost, while the ongoing licensing and maintenance costs related to the solution will be a run spend.

Now, many organisations globally are running Cyber Security Transformation programs to uplift their capabilities in response to the evolving business and cyber threat landscape. These programs are generally multi-year in nature. Things can often change quite quickly from a business and technology perspective in this time, so it's important to be nimble and adapt. However, this may result in unexpected cost impacts where more effort is needed to onboard certain applications to enterprise solutions or new use-cases may be required for existing tooling such as Security Incident and Event Management (SIEM) to enhance logging and monitoring controls. A mechanism to address this formally through the governance of transformation programs is by raising Change Requests where changes to scope and funding can be proposed. For you to be at the top of your cyber leadership game, you need to understand these funding and governance processes to lead your team and help steer programs effectively.

An actionable tip on finances is to develop a good understanding of the timing and mechanics of budgeting cycles in your organisation. This will enable you to plan, adequately prepare and socialise your own requests, business cases and supporting materials before the submission cut-off dates. Typically, there are templates, forms and procedures related to these submissions. Being familiar with them allows you to meaningfully draft and contribute your requests in a structured manner. Identifying the different committees and stakeholders involved in budget approval and strategic decisions enable you to build relationships with them as well as discuss, socialise, and address potential concerns prior to the actual meetings. Being aware of the budget cycles help you get a view of the different areas in your business that are being funded. This is obviously vital to plan your cyber security initiatives since following the money is really the best way to know the business priorities.

Generally, cyber security functions are considered to be a part of shared services. This means that business units contribute to funding the function as they consume the services. As you seek to get an understanding of finances, I encourage you to also get a sense of the pricing models for cyber security. For example, it could be a standard allocation model where all business units pay a flat fee, or it could be a variable model where business units pay based on their consumption. A combination of these is also possible where certain services are flat fee while others could have a variable component. On the topic of services, it is really important that a clear and complete cyber services catalogue is created and maintained. This helps the business understand the different services available to them and is essential to express the value proposition offered through cyber security.

A well-developed service catalogue supported by pricing models helps the organisation understand the potential costs involved - both one-time and ongoing. This will enable your business areas to plan their own budgets and account for the necessary resources needed for adequate security coverage. Also, if you ask the business to deploy a new control or improve an existing process, these may come at a cost to them, so you need to have a good handle on the drivers for the change e.g., risk management, compliance requirement, process improvement and related trade-offs.

Now, the success of any cyber security program is dependent on the tone at the top, which is a fancy term to say visible and consistent support of the executive leadership e.g., C-suite and the Board. The biggest challenge cyber security professionals face in getting executive support is that they are speaking a different language than what the executives understand. It's analogous to me doing a presentation without a translator in my native language Gujarati to a group of people who only speak and understand English. It just won't work. When you speak the business language and frame your cyber security activities in financial and risk terms, you will get both credibility and support from the people you need on your side to achieve success.

Let me give you an example of how I have used the business-aligned approach to influence executives. I was working with a large organisation in the midst of a massive transformation and whose strategy was shifting to a direct-to-consumer model relying heavily on digital channels. I was looking to garner executive support for formalising the cyber security strategy and deployment of controls primarily in the application security areas to support the business strategy shift. Getting executive support was important for multiple reasons, including appropriate prioritisation and sequencing of activities. This matters because, at any given time, an organisation has several in-flight and planned activities. Without necessary prioritisation and sequencing, there is an execution risk even for approved projects and initiatives.

Now, for my presentation with the executives, I had to ensure that they not only understood the importance of what I was suggesting but were also onboard with actively supporting and promoting the recommendations. To be successful here, I needed engagement from both them and their teams. It just couldn't be the cyber function pushing an agenda. It had to be the business understanding the significance of what needed to be done and proactively engaging the cyber team to make it happen.

So, instead of starting my presentation with technical topics such as secure coding, vulnerabilities scanning or penetration testing, which would have likely lost engagement from my target executive audience, I started my presentation by showing how many new users were signing up for the digital channels every day. I also gave a snapshot of how customers and stakeholders were engaging with organisational products and services through digital channels – website, mobile applications, and chatbots. I got this information through working with the right business and technology stakeholders, following the tips provided earlier in this rule. I framed the message to the executives in essentially a couple of slides connecting the dots between the organisational strategy of direct to consumer, the technology strategy of rapid digitisation, and how the cyber security strategy would enable these.

I also provided statistics on attempted attacks on the organisational internet-facing channels and made it real that if our customers can reach us from anywhere, so can the bad actors. Including these statistics was helpful because I had set a business-led foundation for them. They weren't just a bunch of cyber-provided numbers. Rather, they were connected to a strategic business outcome which is where the value lies. I also educated the executives on the simple fact that these days all you need to launch a successful cyber-attack is access to a laptop and a few hundred dollars to buy nefarious services from the dark web. Along with this threat context, I gave them a view of the cyber controls that help mitigate the threat of an external malicious attacker targeting our web-facing applications.

These included controls such as Web Application Firewalls and improving secure coding and testing practices to ensure the secure-by-design principle. I also shared a potential cost optimisation opportunity by highlighting that improving the human factor through training developers could significantly help reduce the cost and effort required to fix penetration testing findings that are typically late and therefore expensive in the process. What helped make the point around cost optimisation even more pronounced was sharing numbers that demonstrated the increasing amount of money being spent on penetration testing-related activities, which were uncovering the same repeated findings that could be addressed more efficiently through early engagement and good secure coding practices. With the threat, controls, and commercial context, I was able to frame the message in a meaningful way by demonstrating how the maturity of key controls directly correlated with the risk posture.

With a clear alignment between business, technology, and risk, I got the support of executive leadership to proceed with the strategy and control implementation. The success of this presentation resulted in the executives inviting me to deliver regular cyber briefings to their own lines of businesses, thus helping me with my objective of seeking active and visible engagement. Since the success of cyber security relies on engagement with key stakeholders, I can safely say that my business-aligned cyber security presentation led to a very healthy outcome with senior leadership and their teams.

Once you understand the business, you must build and foster relationships with the right stakeholders with a focus on becoming a trusted partner to them. Work diligently towards improving any sub-optimal processes or approaches that cause the business to perceive cyber security as a blocking function that stifles innovation and new ideas. Your role is to enable the business to achieve their objectives securely through helping them make informed risk decisions based on well contextualised and articulated information. Some of these stakeholder relationships could be formalised through forums such as cyber security steering committees to discuss cyber risk posture and emerging threats, guide the design and implementation of security controls, address areas of concern, and champion the adoption of security initiatives across lines of businesses. For larger organisations or conglomerates, it's beneficial to have tailored cyber security strategies and risk views that account for the priorities, challenges, and unique nature of the lines of businesses. These business unit-specific strategies should have a clear two-way linkage with the central or group cyber security strategy and program.

I also encourage you to develop an understanding of the different forums and committees that are involved in governing and managing cyber security considerations. These could be risk, compliance, and audit committees, Architecture Review Boards, and/ or dedicated cyber security oversight committees. Familiarise yourself with the terms of reference of these groups.

In my experience, a good starting point for understanding the cyber security governance mechanism is by identifying the accountable executive for cyber security in the organisation and then looking at their reporting structure, their peers, as well as their key stakeholders.

You may be thinking about how this works if one is a mid or junior-level professional and may not have direct communication lines with senior executives. In this case, you start with your immediate leaders and ask for that understanding! So simple, yes? Simple but not easy. In my many years of running and managing cyber programs, I haven't had as many people proactively approach me with a desire to understand the business better as I'd like. However, this number increases after I talk to the teams about the importance of understanding business and its relationships to their success. I hope that this book can serve as that trigger for you in lieu of me being physically present in your organisation. By approaching your leaders with the ask of getting to know the business better, you'll demonstrate your value and, in turn, challenge them to become more effective in their roles. Leadership is an attitude, a growth mindset, and a desire to do things better. You don't need a title or many people reporting to you to be a leader.

Now, cyber security is becoming prominent during Mergers, Acquisitions and Divestiture. When you are aligned with your business, you can play a significant role through early engagement and due diligence. For an acquisition this could involve understanding the nature of the business being acquired and performing the required diligence to determine key cyber risks such as data security, regulatory compliance, etc. For divestiture, it could involve managing risks related to separation of systems and data, sensitive data leakage concerns, disgruntled insiders causing damage, etc. Working closely with your business during these strategic activities will help manage cyber security considerations through the various phases of the deal that involve a lot of organisational change.

Additionally, there is an increasing expectation on organisations to manage cyber security risks and address them adequately as part of their Environmental, Social, and Corporate Governance (ESG) strategy. This is an incredibly positive development in my view, but it is another area that will require a business-aligned cyber security mindset to be truly successful. After all, a good cyber risk management program is entirely dependent on the knowledge of business processes to determine key assets, threats, controls, and the corresponding risk posture.

An exceptional cyber security leader is an individual who can successfully translate between business speak on finances, products, and services with technical details around threats, vulnerabilities, controls, and technology solutions. Someone who can effectively identify and engage with the business stakeholders. Hopefully, this rule provided some ideas on becoming an effective translator and leader. We will continue this theme of a business-aligned cyber security mindset through subsequent rules.

"Take calculated risks. That is quite different from being rash."

— George S. Patton

Recognise that Cyber Security is a Risk Management Exercise

From a business perspective, every dollar spent on cyber security is a dollar that an organisation could be investing in building new products or services and improving them, so it better be spent wisely. This is something that I believe should always be on the mind of cyber security professionals. A risk-based approach facilitates the prudent prioritisation of investments. It is important to recognise that organisations and people invest in cyber security primarily to manage risks in pursuit of their strategic and operational objectives. Exceptional cyber security professionals need to have the ability to understand risks, articulate them, and manage them effectively.

Now, cyber risk management is a vast topic, which has several bodies of knowledge dedicated to itself and I've recommended a few in the resources section. For our current purpose, though, I'd like to focus on the practical aspects of cyber risk and give you some pointers on optimising this key component of cyber security.

You can only understand the risk if you know what you are trying to protect, i.e., the critical services and assets for the organisation. As we covered in Rule 1, understanding the business allows the proper identification of critical assets and what matters most. Organisation's critical assets also depend on the type of industry. For organisations such as financial services, this could be predominantly information systems and data with a major focus on fraud prevention and secure and reliable financial transactions. For the Energy industry, critical assets could include Operational Technology (OT) considerations such as Industrial Control Systems managing power plants where the risks could include physical safety and impact on the delivery of critical energy supplies. Knowing your business and industry well allows you to get this picture. Also, when I use the term critical assets – don't assume I am just talking about Information Technology (IT) or Information Systems. It can also mean OT systems.

While risk management is a detailed topic, the fundamental approach is straightforward – know your assets, understand the threats that apply to them, assess the current state of controls (both in terms of their existence and effectiveness) and corresponding vulnerabilities. Based on the assessment of the current control posture, determine the likelihood and impact of the threats – this is your current risk view. Depending on your organisation's risk appetite there might be a need to mature the controls further to bring the level of residual risk lower than the current state.

Also, when we talk about risk management, it's important to get the language right. Far too often, I see people interchangeably and erroneously use terms such as threats, vulnerabilities, and risks. This can create confusion, especially when dealing with business stakeholders.

So, let's get clear on the terms below:

Threats – The various events that can negatively affect organisations or people. Threats need to be contextualised to be relevant for organisations. E.g., Ransomware is a threat to healthcare organisations but is not a risk by itself.

Vulnerabilities – Weaknesses in people, processes and technology that can be exploited by threat actors to cause damage. Missing patches and poorly trained employees are vulnerabilities but not risks in themselves. Generally, threat actors fall in the below categories:

- External Malicious Actors, including:
  - Cyber criminals with primary motivation being financial gain. The capabilities of these criminals can vary from highly sophisticated individuals and organised crime groups to amateurs. The widespread and easy availability of hacking tools and services including Ransomware-as-a-service, has made the barrier of entry to the shady world of cyber crime really low.
  - Nation-State actors which consist of governments or government-backed organisations with motivations that encompass economic gain, obtaining strategic advantage during conflicts including war-like situations, matters of diplomacy, trade negotiations, and international resolutions.

These actors unsurprisingly have extremely high levels of capabilities and resources.

o Hacktivists who hack or create cyber disruptions for the purpose of making a political or social point. Their capability and resourcing levels can vary depending on the group and their agenda.

- Internal Malicious Actors including disgruntled people in organisations who do bad things to make money or hurt their employer by causing losses and/or embarrassment.

- Non-malicious trusted insiders, including staff, vendors, and third parties who make mistakes or are compromised by malicious actors leading to adverse cyber impacts on organisations.

Controls – People, Processes and Technologies that enable organisations to deliver on their goals by reducing the likelihood and impact of risk events.

Risks – Bringing it all together, when a threat exploits a vulnerability, we have a risk event. These events have the potential to impact organisational objectives – strategic, financial, operational, compliance, and reputational among others. Threats need to be framed in the context of impact and likelihood, accounting for vulnerabilities and controls to inform risk events. An example of a risk event is Ransomware attack on business-critical systems through social engineering or system vulnerability exploitation that causes an outage in excess of maximum tolerable thresholds defined by the organisation. To frame cyber risk scenarios effectively, you need to understand and align with overall organisational risk taxonomy and enterprise risk management processes.

Since I've referred to Ransomware and it is one of the biggest cyber security challenges that all industries are struggling with, let's understand it better. In Ransomware attacks, cyber criminals infect critical systems with malware making them unavailable until a ransom is paid. Lately, the attacks have evolved where criminals also compromise systems with sensitive data and threaten to make them public to put additional pressure for a ransom payment. However, there are no guarantees that systems and data will be made available post ransom payment. While it is a heavily discouraged practice, reality is that many organisations globally have paid ransom to criminals to be able to continue their operations. I can understand the plight of some these organisations especially when impacts are almost catastrophic for them and the people they serve. However, when ransom payments are made, they encourage and further the vicious nature of cybercrime.

Ransomware infection can happen through multiple vectors or but more commonly, it starts with exploiting the human factor through social engineering and tricking people into clicking on malicious links or executing malicious files. It is now recognised that most successful cyber-attacks start with a phishing email. Controls such as effective user education and awareness, multi-factor authentication, patching, email filtering and endpoint security tools will help with reducing the likelihood of ransomware incidents, while others such as mature and tested incident management process, continuity planning, and reliable backups will help with reducing the impact of incidents. Most of these controls are simple hygiene controls. However, implementing and focussing on them can go a long way in addressing the growing menace of ransomware.

Now, let's look at another cyber security scenario through images 1 and 2 in the subsequent pages, which will help explain the relationship and distinction between vulnerabilities, risk events, impacts, and controls. In this example, the risk is a breach of sensitive information leading to several adverse impacts on the organisation.

Impacts
Regulatory Action
Direct and Indirect Financial Losses
Reputation Damage and Lost Trust
Risk Event
Breach of Sensitive Data
Vulnerabilities
Inadequate Third-party Risk Management
Poorly Trained Employees
Unpatched Systems

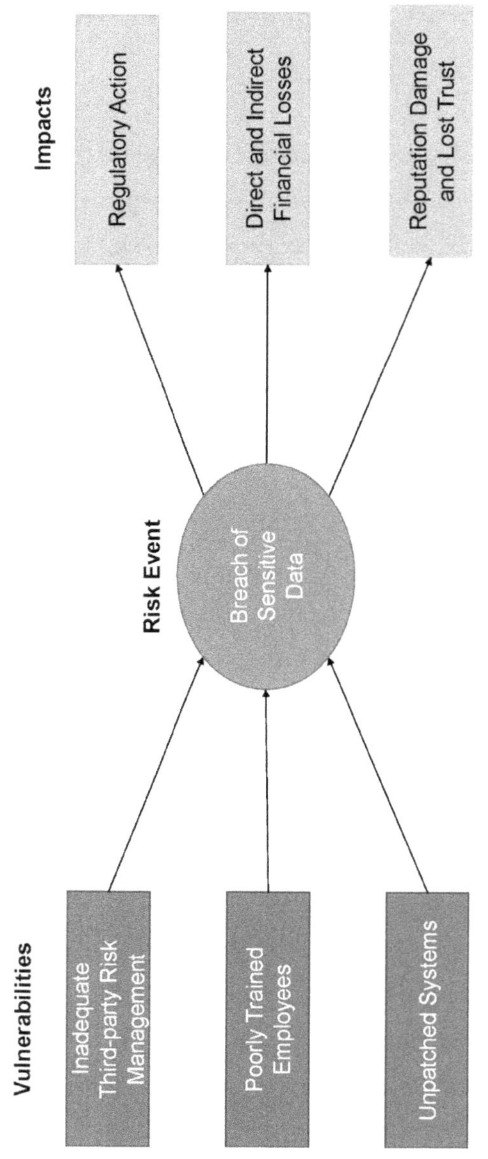

IMAGE 1

When assessing risk scenarios, it is important to identify threat actors that are most relevant to an organisation and its services. For the purpose of our example, the primary relevant threat actors selected are external malicious attackers and non-malicious trusted insiders and partners.

Now, there could be several vulnerabilities that apply in this context, but in our example, we have inadequate third-party risk management processes, poorly trained employees, and systems missing critical patches. Note I haven't called them risks but rather vulnerabilities or weaknesses because that's exactly what they are. It would be a risk when a threat actor exploits the vulnerability leading to an impact. The potential impacts in this example of a sensitive data breach could be the following:

- Regulatory action including fines and other remediation requirements such as Enforceable Undertaking.

- Financial losses caused by the impact on business operations, investigation, response, and remediation activities.

- Reputational damage leading to loss of customer trust and adverse impact on the organisational brand, which could have repercussions on in-progress or potential business deals or product launches.

Vulnerabilities
Controls influencing Likelihood
Risk Event
Controls influencing Impact
Impacts
Inadequate Third-party Risk Management
Poorly Trained Employees
Unpatched Systems
Vendor cyber risk management process
Timely security reviews and ongoing assurance
Awareness and Education
Effective patching processes
Identification of critical information assets
Breach of Sensitive Data
Defensible cyber risk posture
Incident detection and response capability
Tested data breach response and communication plans
Regulatory Action
Direct and Indirect Financial Losses
Reputation Damage and Lost Trust

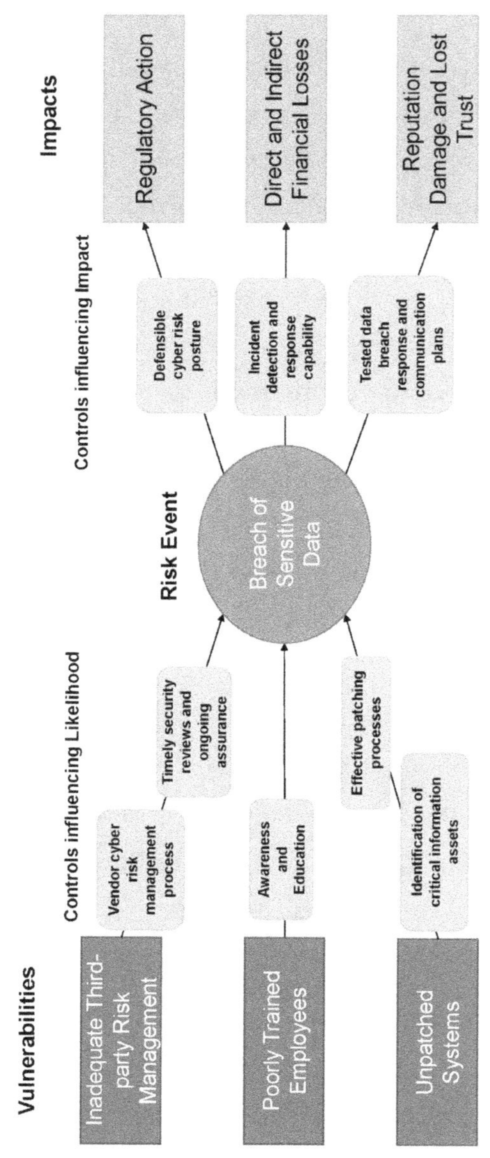

IMAGE 2

The scenario in image 1 represented the inherent risk which is the risk without considering any controls. Now, controls help with reducing the likelihood and impact of vulnerability exploitation by threat actors. By putting a control overlay on image 1, we get image 2.

There are several controls mentioned in image 2, but let's drill down into a vulnerability area so we can make this example more real. We'll pick third-party risk management. This is a very timely topic since the reliance on managed service providers and third-parties is only increasing for many organisations. Cyber criminals are very aware of this and have focussed their nefarious efforts on compromising this vector. After all, isn't it more efficient to compromise one major vendor or managed services provider and through that mechanism gain a potential foothold into their vast customer-base?

We have seen these scenarios play out a fair bit lately, notably the SolarWinds breach among others. SolarWinds is a major IT firm, and its Orion system is used by many organisations to monitor and manage their IT resources. Attackers installed malicious software in the Orion system, which was then sent to its customers through a routine patch. The impact was massive and included organisations, such as Microsoft and major government agencies. I have included links in the resources section of the book for additional information. The resources section also has links for information on another notable supply chain attack – Kaseya.

A good vendor cyber risk management process that includes the following goes a long way in addressing the vulnerability:

- Identifying and tiering all vendors based on information sensitivity, access to the organisational environment, and business criticality.

- Commensurate security assessments which include confirmation of applicable key controls such as encryption, authentication and access management, independent penetration testing, awareness and training, secure backups, etc.

- Legal reviews and contractual clauses which include obligations to report a security or privacy incident promptly, right to audit, maintaining compliance with applicable regulatory requirements and industry good practices.

- Regular monitoring of vendor's security posture based on the relevant tier.

- Established relationships, including defined roles and responsibilities with procurement, vendor governance and legal teams.

In my observation, most organisations rely on one size fits all questionnaires to do security assessments. While it's not necessarily the worst thing, it doesn't really offer as much value in terms of assurance when you consider the effort to benefit ratio of this exercise.

A more prudent approach is targeted and tailored use of these questionnaires with a focus on the relevant threats and getting assurance over the corresponding controls. In some cases, the efforts are well-spent on understanding the vendor's secure software development and management processes, especially if they will play a vital role in your own organisation's operations. The process should also include pragmatically leveraging independent assurance reports such as ISO 27001 with appropriate Statement of Applicability and System and Organisation Controls (SOC) 2 reports. It is important that these reports are reviewed by knowledgeable personnel to ensure proper check and challenge. Increasingly regulators are expecting organisations to not just take these reports at face value but understand and assess their relevance to the organisation.

Technology is also helping with vendor risk management through security rating solutions that offer a real-time view of your vendors' public-facing threat posture. This provides you with an indicator of potential risk as well as visibility into your vendor's vendors, so essentially fourth parties. There are also trusted groups and exchanges forming where a vendor assessment can be leveraged by multiple organisations considering doing business with them as opposed to all of them doing essentially the same thing individually. While not perfect, these developments can help augment and improve ongoing assurance of the supplier's security posture.

It should be noted that the goal of cyber security isn't to eliminate all risks, incidents, and breaches. That's just not realistic. The intent is to manage and reduce these risks, be resilient in the face of threats and allow the business of the organisation to continue effectively. When incidents do occur, a defensible cyber security program built on a strong foundation of risk management and associated controls framework goes a long way in giving confidence to regulators as well as other stakeholders. Tested incident detection and response plans and capabilities reduce the impact of incidents. With the ever-increasing volume and sophistication of cyber threats, senior leaders and the general public are starting to acknowledge that a breach can occur despite an organisation's best efforts.

However, they do expect a coordinated and trustworthy response and remediation mechanism to address the incident or breach. It is paramount to communicate honestly and transparently through this time. Handled well, incidents can also lead to silver linings in the longer term.

Now, the design and operating effectiveness of the controls will dictate the residual risk of scenarios such as the one described in the images. This risk should then be treated as per the organisational risk appetite. Simply put, risk appetite is the amount of risk an organisation is prepared to accept in pursuit of its mission. The options to treat the residual risk could include further control enhancements in the form of mitigation, risk acceptance, and risk avoidance by discontinuing the risky activity or risk transfer through means such as insurance. Regardless of the option chosen, the ultimate responsibility for cyber risk still rests with the organisation.

Careful attention should be paid to the cyber risk appetite expressed by the organisation. If the cyber risk appetite appears to be misaligned with organisational growth ambitions or practical realities, it should be reviewed and adjusted in consultation with business, technology, risk, and other relevant functions. I suggest challenging broad qualitative statements such as low appetite for cyber risks with some tangible examples and associated cost-benefit trade-offs to ascertain if they are fit for purpose. These can be expressed in the context of loosening or tightening standards and requirements in areas such as patching, supplier security assessment, security testing approaches etc. For example, if an organisation wants to expand quickly through innovation and rapidly introduce new functionalities in its online offerings while aggressively leveraging Software as a Service (SaaS) and digital channels, security requirements that are aligned with a very low risk appetite may prove onerous and counter-productive to the swift growth ambitions and may need to be revised.

As a practical tip, organisations generally do a reasonable job of risk management around financial, operational, and compliance risks, as these are driven by regulatory requirements for many industries. These risks are handled in accordance with the enterprise risk framework. It is vital that cyber risk is also clearly called out and incorporated into the enterprise risk framework. This will allow for a consistent set of criteria to be applied for assessing the likelihood and impact of cyber risks in terms of financial, reputational, customer, legal and other measures. As always, if you aren't aware of these processes in your organisation, converse with your leader or immediate manager. These are important for you to understand no matter what your cyber security role is – technical, governance or management.

As far as possible, the goal should be to quantify the risk in terms of financials. You are in a better position to present this picture if you have the business insights and understand the architecture and dependencies of key information assets to other systems. This can help you talk the language of probabilities of likelihoods and impacts. For example, if you are doing a risk assessment for a critical business application and understand the revenue generated through it, the overall control environment, and the threat landscape, you can then assign probabilities of likelihoods in percentage terms. For example, in a weaker control environment, there could be an approximately 80% likelihood of a successful cyber incident impacting critical business applications that can result in a loss of a certain amount of dollars. The likelihood and impact of this scenario can be reduced to a lower probability, such as 30% and a lesser dollar amount respectively, by proportionately investing in the maturity of cyber security controls. Ensure that your investment ask captures both one-time uplift change costs and any ongoing run costs as a result of the recommendation. Framing investment requests against specific cyber risk scenarios clearly indicate the cost and benefit trade-off. Articulating a problem and associated solution in this way allows the business to make good-informed decisions.

The key here is to not get overly concerned with perfection. Don't let perfect be the enemy of the good. Your financial impact estimation need not be accurate to the nth degree. Ranges are acceptable.

Just remember that financials make sense to decision-makers; it's the language that is the most tangible. Giving them a sense of potential financial losses along with other considerations such as compliance, contractual and reputational impacts make for a more compelling discussion than mere subjective, qualitative statements. This makes cyber security a value add, which is exactly what we want. The good news is that there have been several improvements in the industry recently, with more cyber risk quantification frameworks and tools being introduced. I have included links related to these in the resources section that can help you with this exercise.

Often during my public speaking and social media interactions, I get questions about how you get the senior leadership to pay attention to cyber security, especially for less regulated sectors and small to medium organisations. While each situation is probably different with organisational constraints and culture, including cyber risk into the existing organisational risk taxonomy, processes and reporting cadence is an extremely effective step. This will help with a voice and attention at the Executive table. The cyber risk profile then can serve as an anchor against which you can track and manage the progress of your cyber security efforts.

I am a big advocate of a clear and tangible linkage of investments, programs, and operational activities with relevant cyber risks that account for the business-critical assets and processes. Every activity performed by a cyber security function, or any tool introduced should have a linkage to the overall cyber risk profile of the organisation.

"If you can't measure it, you can't improve it."

— **Peter Drucker**

Measure it

What gets measured gets managed and what gets managed delivers value. That's just how it is, how it has been, and how it will be. As exceptional professionals, the objective should always be to deliver value to our organisations. Naturally, this extends to cyber security. Well-defined and relevant metrics are key to measuring the progress of cyber security initiatives against goals and objectives.

A common problem with cyber security metrics in many organisations is that they aren't tailored for the right audience, nor are they measuring the things that truly matter. For example, metrics such as the number of alerts triggered by an endpoint security solution or the number of people attending security awareness training sessions are good for operational teams to improve the effectiveness of their efforts but offer no strategic insights into the security posture to senior executives and board directors.

Good strategic metrics have a close correlation to the material risks for the organisation and should drive decisions. They are focussed on critical assets and services. This criticality should be derived from factors including the business impacts related to confidentiality, integrity, and availability of the assets and services. These impacts must also account for sensitivity of the data involved. Other factors that impact the criticality ratings are internet exposure, the interconnectivity of these assets to other assets in the environment, regulatory requirements, and hosting arrangements.

Critical assets derived from the aforementioned factors can then be considered crown jewels for the organisation. Identification of these assets helps with prioritisation of resources and protection requirements. Ultimately, if everything is important, then nothing is really important.

Good strategic metrics bring to life ongoing protection for the critical assets. Instead of talking about the number of vulnerabilities, penetration test findings or number of alerts, examples of a potentially useful metrics are:

- percentage of critical internet-facing applications with critical patches applied within defined timelines.

- percentage of critical internet-facing applications protected by the enterprise Web Application Firewall that monitors and filters out malicious traffic to the applications.

- percentage of critical internet-facing applications with Multi-factor Authentication enabled to address the risk of compromise of a single factor such as passwords.

- percentage of critical vendors who have undergone security assessments.

The value of these strategic metrics improves significantly if you can break them down by key business areas with associated financial impacts. For example, the percentage of critical patches not applied in a timely manner for infrastructure hosting the organisational flagship website that is used by customers to manage accounts and make payments. This metric will get the attention of the executives because it has a direct linkage with a critical business process and cash flow. Following the steps in Rule 1 should help you articulate what the potential financial losses could be if the flagship website was impacted.

A practical way to think about metrics is to account for both coverage and effectiveness measures. So, metrics focussed on patching are effectiveness-based since they track conformance with established processes and standards. While metrics such as the number of critical applications onboarded to enterprise Security Incident and Event Management (SIEM), or Privileged Access Management (PAM) solutions are good coverage metrics. It's prudent to have a healthy balance of these presented to the executives to give them a holistic picture of the state of current controls but also the deployment status of newly uplifted controls.

A good balance also involves including both leading and lagging indicators. Metrics focussed on the number of incidents in the last quarter is a lagging indicator, which gives an after-the-fact picture to guide actions and reviews. Metrics that provide information on the number of days it takes to patch business-critical systems can serve as a leading indicator that gives a forward-looking view of potential risk.

Now, a good way to establish metrics is by taking the SMART approach. SMART is a goal-setting technique that has been around for several decades now.

SMART stands for Specific, Measurable, Achievable or Actionable, Relevant, and Time-bound. For example, a SMART metric for an organisation with a massive reliance on direct-to-consumer digital channels such as eCommerce business could relate to secure-by-design of web applications. Uplifting secure coding practices would be highly relevant here, and the SMART metric would look something like this - after 6-months of Open Web Application Security Project (OWASP) top 10 secure coding training for developers working on critical applications, the percentage of security defects related to the top 10 vulnerabilities found later in life cycle during penetration testing would decrease by 20%.

The metric is **Specific** with a focus on OWASP top 10 secure coding training for developers working on critical applications. It is **Measurable** with a 20% decrease in the percentage of security defects. It is **Achievable** – there is a way to reasonably obtain this information through a combination of training completion statistics and penetration testing report trends. It is **Relevant** because it's tied directly to the cyber risk for an eCommerce organisation. It is **Time-bound** with a 6-months timeline.

This way of measuring the success of initiatives is helpful in focussing resources as well as demonstrating progress through tangible means to the senior executives.

Now that we have covered what good looks like from a metrics perspective, I want to focus on understanding the importance of maturity and benchmarking. First, let's just explore what senior executives and boards are interested in from a cyber perspective. These areas typically revolve around questions such as, Are we managing our risks appropriately? Are we compliant with regulations? Are we investing appropriately? Is the organisation moving in the right direction? There might be some other areas, but largely, the interest revolves around the items I mentioned. Well-designed and implemented controls programs, along with appropriate assurance and reporting activities are vital to covering all the main bases for senior executives and boards.

As far as possible, I recommend leveraging international or well-recognised frameworks and standards to establish your own control set. Examples of these frameworks include the NIST Cyber Security Framework (CSF) and ISO 27001.

In some cases, your industry vertical or regulatory guidance may inform the adoption of certain frameworks, e.g., the Australian Energy Sector Cyber Security Framework (AESCSF) for the Energy sector. You could also leverage standards such as Payment Card Industry Data Security Standard (PCI DSS). There are plenty of frameworks and standards you can easily find on the Internet, and I have included some in the resources section. It is worth noting that no framework by itself is a silver bullet. You must always consider its application and utility in the context of your organisational environment. It can be quite useful to derive benefits by combining good practices from multiple frameworks and standards.

After selecting the appropriate frameworks, you must ensure that you have identified key and supporting controls for your risk scenarios. For example, multi-factor authentication, training, patching, endpoint and network security, and Web Application Firewall could be some of the key controls for threat related to an external malicious attacker compromising internet-facing systems through social engineering or system exploitation. Post designing and tailoring your controls framework, you should establish a periodic process to measure the maturity of controls.

Now, there are quite a few maturity models you can leverage but keeping it simple – you can typically measure your controls on a scale of 1-5. In general:

Level 1 represents an ad-hoc set of security practices with very limited or no documentation, standardisation, or organisational communication.

Level 2 represents more documentation and organisational awareness, with some level of standardisation emerging in pockets of the organisation but still limited.

Level 3 represents controls formally documented, implemented, and standardised across the organisation.

Level 4 represents controls being regularly measured and managed besides being standardised.

Level 5 represents a state where the security controls are actively being optimised and automated.

As you can see from the above, each level is an uplift over the previous one, and you typically need to reach a level before you can hit the next. The same maturity approach can be used for tool implementations where initially, the focus could be on a roll-out to proof-of-concept applications, and then the solution is progressively standardised and expanded to the broader organisation. At the higher levels of maturity, these tools must be actively tuned based on threat intelligence and internal risk environment with a good degree of automation to avoid inefficiencies and clunky manual processes.

The advantage of an international framework such as NIST Cyber Security Framework (CSF) is that it categorises controls in five easily understood domains – identify, protect, detect, respond, and recover. This allows organisations to assess their maturity across each domain and with NIST CSF being an international framework, it allows for benchmarking of their maturity relative to their peers globally and locally. Benchmarking information is very useful when conversing with executives and boards. These data points indicate to them the health of the cyber program relative to the industry. It also serves as an important tool in communicating the story of your cyber security journey. With benchmarking and maturity data points, you can demonstrate progress and frame a call to action on areas that need attention.

It's worth noting that there isn't a right or wrong answer to what level of control maturity an organisation should target. This depends completely on the business objectives and organisational risk appetite. For example, an organisation operating within cost constraints trying to rapidly leverage SaaS and public cloud (e.g., AWS or Azure) may have a greater risk appetite in pursuit of its mission and be willing to accept a maturity level of 3 with consequent benefits and gaps. While another organisation in a highly regulated environment with significant investment capability and low-risk appetite might target a maturity rating of over 4 in pursuit of its mission.

Organisations could also target individual domain ratings accounting for benchmarking data. So, they may aim to be at maturity level 4 for Identify, Protect and Recover domains and maturity level 3.5 for Detect and Respond. Again, there isn't a right or wrong answer if it's a well-thought-out decision working with the business and organisational risk processes.

As a practical tip, I suggest that you take a pragmatic approach to controls including policies and standards. There should be avenues and processes to seek informed exemptions with compensating controls where it is impractical or infeasible to implement the recommended controls. These exemptions should be tracked and risk-assessed appropriately to ensure proper checks and balances. Pragmatism is the name of the game when it comes to being a good partner to your business. Also, if you notice that there are continuous exemptions being sought from your recommended controls, perhaps it's time for you to revisit their design and gauge if these are indeed fit-for-purpose for your organisation.

For smaller organisations with limited cyber resources, I recommend focussing on hygiene controls– access management including password security, enabling multi-factor authentication, user education, patching, regular backups, and working with reputed third parties with regards to data and systems. Leverage frameworks and standards to design the hygiene controls and start with tracking and reporting their maturity to guide investments and prioritisation. I have included some practical cyber resources for small and medium-sized businesses in the resources section.

In conclusion, I hope the importance of measuring the maturity of your control posture and the utility of benchmarking against an international standard is clear. This provides information and confidence to your senior leadership on how your security program is tracking and its performance relative to your peers. This also helps with proportionate investment discussions when you're considering your spend profile.

"Humanity has the stars in its future, and that future is too important to be lost under the burden of juvenile folly and ignorant superstition."

— Isaac Asimov

Address the Human factor

This rule is perhaps the one I am the most passionate about. So much so that I dedicated a full book to this topic – 7 Rules to Influence Behaviour and Win at Cyber Security Awareness. I'd recommend looking at it if you'd like a deeper dive into building effective and efficient cyber security awareness programs. However, for our current purposes, I want to touch on some key points you should have in mind as a cyber security leader about the human factor.

Firstly, it is important to recognise that the vast majority of cyber security incidents occur due to human errors and mistakes.

Most credible industry reports attribute around 80% of cyber incidents and breaches to the human factor! I have included links to some of these reports in the resources section. Incidents related to the human factor include social engineering, misconfigurations, and not following recommended organisational processes. Even a lot of so-called sophisticated attacks have a human factor at their core. E.g., tricking someone into clicking on a malicious link in a phishing email leading to malware (including ransomware) installation and large-scale system compromise. Another common one is exploiting the human tendency to be lazy and use the same weak password for multiple accounts where if one of their accounts is compromised, all other accounts are also put at risk.

With such a massive reliance on the human factor, we must acknowledge that cyber security is fundamentally a human problem. After all, cyber security and technology are for humans and by humans. No matter how great a piece of technology is but if humans aren't operating it or consuming it effectively, it'll result in rather sub-optimal outcomes.

So, when cyber security is a human problem, we need to understand how humans learn, in order to influence their behaviour and embed good secure practices in people's daily lives. Studies have shown us that humans don't learn well from fear tactics and bad news. Let's look at the image 3 taken from renowned author and professor of cognitive neuroscience, Dr. Tali Sharot's famous presentation on human learning and change (TEDx Talks 2014).

The image is based on comprehensive scientific studies [(Moutsiana, Garrett, Clarke, Lotto, Blakemore, and Sharot 2013)], [(Chowdhury, Sharot, Wolfe, Düzel, Dolan 2014)] that show across various age groups, people are more receptive to the information they consider favourable than information they don't want to hear. Essentially, through the various age groups, the ability to learn from good news such as positive reinforcement and aspirations always does better than the ability to learn from bad news such as warnings and fear tactics.

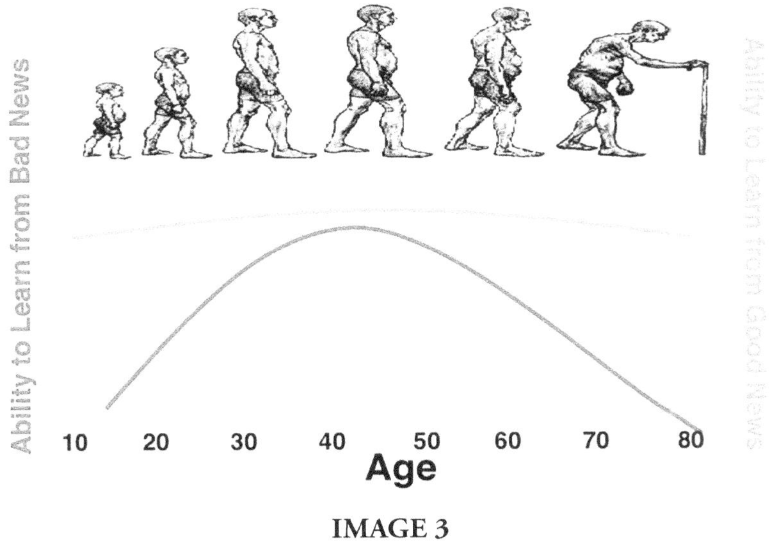

IMAGE 3

So, in my view, while relying on fear might get people's initial attention, it does little to change behaviour in the long term. It doesn't stick. We should keep this in mind when running cyber security education sessions or promoting security collateral. Let's avoid starting every conversation by using the fear card of breaches and incidents. Fear can freeze people and cause them to act irrationally. The bizarre behaviour we noticed at the start of COVID-19 pandemic where people were fighting in supermarkets over toilet papers and hoarding them is a classic example of how fear can make otherwise good people act in a disturbing manner. Using the fear card excessively and giving people no sense of control makes them apathetic or freezes them into inaction. This is the worst thing we can do when we rely a lot on engagement from our stakeholders to succeed.

Also, people use technology to make their lives better, and so do businesses to make their products and services better. The role of technology became so much more prominent during the COVID-19 pandemic, where it allowed people to connect with their loved ones, continue businesses and even allowed for some respite through entertainment in the midst of unprecedented situations such as lockdowns, border closures and an overall environment of high uncertainty. When cyber security comes across being a hindrance to these aspirations through negative messaging, it is already an uphill and a losing battle. Not where you ever want to be. Remember, the vast majority of people want to do the right thing, so we need to make it easier for them to do so through effective and regular education.

Let's replace fear with things that work and appeal to human aspirations, such as enablement of organisation's mission and who they serve, and frame cyber security as an enabler to that mission. Give people a sense of control by giving them valuable insights and options on what they can do to reduce risk and stay secure. Use humour, healthy competition, gamification, and analogies instead of the same old boring one-time mandatory trainings. Competitions such as phishing email writing, scavenger hunts, cyber mascot or logo design challenges are all good and exciting ways to engage your organisation. These require no specific technical expertise to participate.

Phishing simulation exercises, when done well and not driven by a negative mindset, can be an effective mechanism to gauge awareness of your organisation. By negative mindset, I am referring to ineffective punishments such as getting people to repeat boring-lengthy one size fits all training when they fall for the simulated message. The same training, by the way, that didn't help them in the first place. A better, more effective way is to have a compassionate touch and share a learning moment where you assure them that they have fallen for a simulated phishing message, but it's a safe environment and an educational opportunity. Point out what they missed in the phishing message and make yourself available to help if they have questions. If the same people repeatedly fail the exercise, then you can do a dedicated education session with them to understand where your awareness efforts can improve and help them further. Despite these efforts, if you still notice no improvements, consequence management could be your potential course of action. It must, however, be the last and least preferred option.

With phishing simulation campaigns, I'd recommend you frame success as driving an increase in the reporting rate as opposed to just measuring the click rate. Click rate refers to the number of people who click on the phishing email. An increase in reporting rates is a positive, proactive indicator where your people are taking action to help the overall organisation.

Another positive way to get people to pay attention to your educational efforts and retain that information is through the use of analogies.

An example of a cyber security analogy is a picture of a cute puppy with a toothbrush and toothpaste with a message that as cute as the puppy is, you wouldn't use the same toothbrush to brush your teeth and his. Why would you use the same password for multiple accounts, which can include something as serious as your banking account and less sensitive like a website you subscribed to get coupons. Gently pointing out that bad practices, while easy, are still really bad. As we know, with weak shared passwords, if one account is compromised, everything else is also now at risk. In fact, credential stuffing attacks where bad actors try to gain unauthorised access through trying multiple passwords from lists of compromised user credentials are one of the biggest attack vectors today.

Another example is a picture of jewellery and a wallet with a lot of money kept unattended in a public area. The analogy and message shared with the picture is that you wouldn't leave your physical valuables unprotected in public. Why then leave your devices unlocked and unattended? Pointing out that the sensitive information on our devices is equally or even more important than physical valuables. This information could include everything from our bank account details, emails, corporate data, family photos, personally identifiable information, passwords, etc.

I have also used analogies to demonstrate the value of cyber security. One of these include thinking of cyber security as brakes in cars. While it may seem counter intuitive, brakes actually allow cars to go much faster since there is confidence that the car can be stopped safely in case of danger. Without this ability, people would be driving cars much slower to avoid crashes. Similarly, good cyber security practices give confidence to organisations to pursue their ambitions and objectives at pace and scale.

Analogies like these will create more memorable imagery in your audience's mind and hopefully help embed secure practices more than a boring wall of text in an email.

I'd also encourage a committed focus on role-based and just-in-time training as opposed to a one-size-fits-all approach. Training for users with privileged access, such as system administrators and developers writing code for your organisation will look different than it is for people in finance. For the former roles, you'd focus on areas such as credential and access management, secure coding principles, etc., while for the latter, you'd focus more on phishing and payroll diversion attacks. Payroll diversion attacks are where criminals use social engineering tactics to redirect payments from legitimate accounts to those controlled by them.

Just-in-time training helps create long-term behavioural changes since it's based on the idea of helping people solve a problem exactly when they experience it. For example, a just-in-time tip of using password managers when someone is trying to reset a password they have forgotten or needs changing is much more likely to increase adoption of the tool than merely including it in a mandatory training with a host of other topics.

Another tip I'd like to offer for promoting positive behavioural change is to make a personal connection of cyber security to people's lives. Help them understand that regardless of their job title, they are all Chief Information Security Officers of their own homes. The safety and security of their families online rely on them being aware of good cyber security practices. Teaching them to be safe at home will bring positive behaviours to work.

Ultimately, it's a culture of a secure mindset we want to foster. A security culture where everyone in the organisation understands their role and does their part in promoting a more secure outcome. A culture where there is transparency, and people feel empowered and encouraged to report cyber incidents, near-misses or mistakes is an important indicator of the organisational attitude towards security. More people proactively engaging the cyber team and reporting suspicious events should be celebrated.

A good security culture also includes people exhibiting good practices on a daily basis as part of their regular work. For example, a person in finance spotting a phishing email and reporting it promptly, a person in People and Culture using a password manager to ensure they don't have the same weak password being used across different accounts, business leaders ensuring that they are making an informed decision on proceeding with a product feature which could have security implications or a technology leader appropriately balancing good hygiene practice such as patching, configuration management and backups against other demands. A good security culture also enables business teams to ensure that supply chain risks are well managed when engaging a start-up to work on or handle critical organisational assets.

You can promote and reinforce this culture by getting senior executive and leadership support. Get your senior leaders to actively walk the talk and encourage good secure behaviours. This can include them calling out the importance of cyber security practices in all-company updates. This message becomes even more powerful when backed by senior leaders themselves demonstrating good practices such as using password managers, reminding people how to report suspicious events, and visually wearing lanyards and badges to mitigate risks of tailgating and unauthorised physical access.

You can help your senior leaders understand cyber security better through tabletop or simulation exercises where they get to experience the real-world implications of their decisions during a cyber security incident. The simulation exercises can include realistic threat scenarios eventuating, such as ransomware and contain several decisions that need to be made as the fictitious scenario unfolds. These decisions can be around when a formal incident declaration must be made and by whom, which organisations and partners should the information be shared, etc. The exercise can also test the adequacy of steps outlined in the existing incident response process and specifically the ransomware incident playbook if one exists. These can also highlight the need for organisational leadership to formalise positions regarding ransom payments and whether any negotiation will be considered with the criminals in exceptional circumstances. As you can imagine, experiencing these simulations can serve as a really strong incentive for senior leadership to be across the health of their cyber security programs. This makes future conversations with them on risks, investments, and control maturity a lot more engaging and fruitful. You can tailor the duration and level of detail for the exercises depending on the audience and your objective. I have included some links in the resources section to help you with ideas and scenarios for tabletop exercises.

We also need to think about evolving cyber security awareness and communication beyond just training on areas such as phishing, passwords, and policies as important as these are. We need to ensure that the organisation knows how and why to consume the cyber services being offered.

A practical way to achieve this is by running sessions that showcase the cyber security services and the team's work. This can include information on how the team delivers third-party risk management, security consulting, vulnerability management, threat management, etc. Through these showcases, you can also educate your organisation on topics such as differences between a full penetration test and an automated vulnerability scan and which should be used when. These will help your stakeholders engage with you in a more informed manner. I think you'll be pleasantly surprised by the interest you get from your organisation. Many people want to know more about how cyber security works since it has featured so prominently in the public domain

When it comes to educating people in your organisation on different aspects of cyber security and your services, you don't have to do this alone. You must harness the power of allies such as other assurance functions, including privacy, risk, legal, procurement, audit, fraud, and compliance. These functions have a close relationship with cyber security and can serve as excellent partners to cascade your message. I also suggest running joint showcases with these teams so you can give an end-to-end picture of how a supplier security assessment process works with the inclusion of the procurement and legal teams as well to talk about their roles. You can also run joint sessions with fraud teams and show how cyber threat intelligence and operations teams work with fraud teams to investigate and address anomalous events. These joint sessions can help you reach more people and strengthen working relationships with your key organisational partners. Make sure that every session includes information on how stakeholders and people in the organisation can best engage with you and utilise your services.

A quick tip on means of engagement - leveraging automation and digital channels such as workflow systems and chatbots can help with efficiencies in your service delivery. These should certainly be harnessed to their maximum, practical potential. However, the importance of a trusted human face that the business can directly contact and engage with cannot be underestimated. So, I encourage you to keep that in mind as you design your engagement model.

Now, advances in Artificial Intelligence and Machine Learning have caused a positive impact in a host of areas such as fraud detection, shopping experiences, healthcare, image, and speech recognition, among others. However, they have also increased avenues for social engineering and disinformation through things like deep fakes. Deep fakes essentially leverage Artificial Intelligence to create very realistic looking but fake media (images, videos, etc.) of people for nefarious purposes. Currently, email and SMS-based phishing and scams continue to create major challenges for organisations and individuals. Deep Fakes have the potential to make these far worse. While technology will help in protecting people and organisations against these attacks, the importance of human critical thinking is irreplaceable here.

To further add to the importance of critical thinking, remote working and working on the move, which were increasing at a rapid pace before the COVID-19 pandemic anyway, have now become the norm. This change also means there isn't a traditional corporate network perimeter anymore, and pure reliance on technical security controls isn't the answer. Humans, with their critical thinking, are the strongest security control. This is precisely why we need to keep the human factor at the heart of everything we do in cyber security.

"Without strategy, execution is aimless. Without execution, strategy is useless."

— Morris Chang

Understand the Design and Execution of Cyber Security Strategies

A strategy is essentially a holistic and coordinated approach to achieving the desired outcome. A fit-for-purpose strategy forms the basis of a good cyber security program. An important characteristic of a worthy strategy is being nimble and able to accommodate changes in situations around it. Well rounded cyber security leaders and professionals need to have the knowledge of design and execution of these strategies.

This helps them see the big picture and align their activities in a structured manner that delivers value to their organisations.

Through the prior rules, we've covered several elements that go into building an effective cyber security strategy. These are the business drivers, technology landscape and principles, regulatory and compliance requirements, relevant cyber threats and risks, capability, and capacity of the organisation.

For a cyber security strategy to succeed, it needs to have a clear linkage with business and technology strategies.

Business drivers, including organisational culture and governance frameworks, are paramount to designing any security strategy. Business goals of going direct to consumer through digital channels, getting listed or de-listed on stock exchanges, expanding internationally into new jurisdictions, and upcoming acquisitions or divestments are all things with significant implications on cyber security and associated threats.

At a high level, cyber threat scenarios are similar across industries, and I have included some below. However, the impact and focus of these scenarios are derived from the nature of the business.

General Cyber Threat Scenarios:

- External malicious attacker compromising information assets leading to unauthorised data exposure, tampering and/or system unavailability.
- Internal malicious attacker compromising or tampering with information assets.
- Third-party or supplier security weakness or compromise leading to an adverse impact on the organisation.
- Accidental data exposure through mistakes and misconfigurations.
- Brand impersonation leading to scams and other adverse impacts on customers and stakeholders.

Let's consider the following examples to understand how a type of business influences the relevance of cyber threat scenarios.

For an eCommerce company, the availability of its flagship website where customers purchase products is imperative. If the primary website is unavailable due to a denial-of-service type attack, there is an immediate impact on the revenue. Confidentiality is also important to ensure customers' personal and financial details are managed appropriately and are visible only to authorised personnel. Any violation of confidentiality can directly affect customers' relationships and future business with the organisation.

For a healthcare provider with limited reliance on external-facing digital channels but a significant healthcare record database, the integrity and availability of its records take on an important role. Integrity is ensuring information is not tampered with. Essentially, you don't want records that inform critical medical decisions to be based on anything other than complete accuracy. Here, the availability of its public-facing website, which provides general information, and some educational resources, is less important. However, if the internal systems related to patient records and medical procedures are locked out and unavailable due to a ransomware-type attack, the impact can be massive both financially, but more importantly to people's lives and health.

In both scenarios above, confidentiality, integrity, and availability are all relevant. However, the nature and magnitude of their importance can be different.

Now, customers of organisations with well-established and public-facing brands are often targeted through brand-impersonation attacks where criminals fake correspondence to swindle people of their hard-earned money or sensitive information. In some cases, this malicious activity can take the form of a fake website or social media accounts with very similar names and branding of the spoofed entity. For these organisations, cyber security strategy and controls need to account for brand monitoring, customer education, and effective communication to address the threat. However, this wouldn't be the most pressing scenario for organisations that don't have a high public profile or are niche providers serving a select group of clients.

Therefore, a cyber security strategy needs to apply the strategic threat modelling overlay to identify the more pressing scenarios. I have included some threat modelling links in the resources section that can help. Also, ensure that key controls for the scenarios that matter are appropriately addressed and prioritised. Strategies anchored against managing a well-formulated current and target-state cyber risk position generally do very well in terms of getting senior executive support. Leverage information shared in rules 1, 2, and 3 for this exercise.

Now, the technology landscape and associated drivers are other vital components of the strategy. For example, an organisation with workloads primarily in the cloud (e.g., Amazon Web Services (AWS), Microsoft Azure, Google Cloud Platform) or those that were born in the cloud have a different security approach from a technology and process perspective than those with a lot of legacy applications and in-house hosted infrastructure in traditional data centres. With cloud services, there is an element of the shared responsibility model where certain aspects of computing, databases, and network might be managed by the cloud provider while others are the responsibility of the customer. The visibility and ownership of the technology stack also vary, which influences the design and implementation of security controls such as identity and access management, vulnerability and incident management, backup and recovery, logging and monitoring, and protective technologies at network and application layers. There are some native protections offered by cloud providers, such as those against denial-of-service attacks, which may be missing in the on-premises environments. These would need to factor into the security strategy. Additionally, the technical skills required by the security team will also be impacted by the technology landscape. These could include specific skills relevant to the cloud providers' services and architectures.

Also, some organisations' technology landscape leans heavily towards a SaaS model. The approach to application security in this context is very different than organisations which do a lot of application development or customisation internally. These considerations include technology controls such as code scanning, Web Application Firewalls, and people controls such as maintaining a secure coding program.

Furthermore, principles set by the technology strategy have material impacts on cyber security strategy and architecture. For example, if the technology strategy supported by enterprise architecture outlines preference for specific vendors as part of efficiency and cost considerations, it directly influences the inclusion of tools and processes that forms part of the cyber security architecture. Technology strategy principles around building systems vs buying them, heavy customisation or using out-of-the-box features for solutions also affect how cyber security controls would be designed and monitored. As customisation and functionality increases, the cyber threat surface typically also increases.

Compliance and Regulatory drivers are other crucial inputs into a cyber security strategy and architecture that supports it. For example, in Australia, the financial services sector is heavily regulated. Australian Prudential Regulatory Authority (APRA) Cross-industry Prudential Standard (CPS) 234 sets the tone for the financial services sector in the country regarding expectations from cyber security programs. This includes roles and responsibilities of the board and executives, a commensurate risk management program, incident management and notification requirements, among others. Now, for the Energy sector in Australia, the Australian Energy Market Operator (AEMO) encourages the adoption of Australian Energy Sector Cyber Security Framework (AESCSF). AESCSF has a major focus on Operational Technology besides Information Technology. This requires a different approach to cyber security controls and risks than in the financial services sector. Foundational security practices such as patching are quite different in the OT world than in the IT world, especially when it comes to the cadence, frequency, and change impact of the exercise. A lot of legacy OT systems weren't designed with the modern digital world and threats in mind. Also, these purpose-built systems typically have longer lifespans than IT systems, thus necessitating a more focussed strategic approach to asset management. The prescriptive nature of the regulations and recommended practices also tend to be quite different and play a role in the overall design of the strategic roadmap. Additionally, data sovereignty requirements driven by regulations such as Global Data Protection Regulation (GDPR) also have material implications on security processes such as third-party risk management.

A key feature of regulations relates to incident and breach reporting. There is a trend globally where regulators in different countries and sectors are setting expectations on incident reporting timelines. Definition of what constitutes an incident or breach is not always consistent across the different regulatory regimes. Clearly, these requirements and considerations need to factor into your cyber security strategy and stakeholder management processes. Typically, in larger organisations, there are multiple teams involved with regulator interactions. These include risk, compliance, regulatory affairs, legal, and business representatives. A streamlined and effective process for incident management and reporting needs consultation and agreement between these different areas.

Hopefully, I've made clear the significant impact of regulations and recommended practices on organisational cyber security controls. Also, boards and executives always want to ensure that all material regulatory commitments and expectations are being met and addressed appropriately, thus further contributing to their importance.

We've looked at the inputs that go into building a good cyber security strategy. Now let's look at some elements material to the execution of the strategy. After all, strategy without execution is just a wish list.

One of the important aspects of strategy execution involves designing the appropriate sourcing models for delivering cyber security services. Sourcing models include but aren't limited to insourcing, outsourcing, hybrid, contractor-heavy or persistent teams with permanent employees. These models are influenced, and in turn, influence the capacity and capability of the organisation. In my view, the more commodity-type cyber security services such as penetration testing, where the market has better capabilities that can be leveraged and scaled more efficiently, are potentially good candidates to be out-sourced or co-sourced with services providers. I have similar thoughts on threat intelligence services.

When engaging with service providers, it is critical that there is careful development and understanding of Service Level Agreements (SLAs). These SLAs need to be aligned with the organisational risk appetite and commercial realities. Ambiguities in roles and responsibilities of capabilities being delivered and their timelines is one of the more common reasons contributing to sub-optimal or adverse security outcomes. Working with the procurement, vendor governance and legal teams closely will help you get the most out of strategic sourcing arrangements with your service providers.

Along with sourcing models, operating models for cyber security services are also an important factor. Good operating models inform the roles and responsibilities within the organisation related to cyber security controls. For example, what role does the cyber security team play in network security. Do they play a governance role of establishing the policies, standards, and reporting requirements while the run component of technology is handled by the network team? Or does the cyber security team have the responsibility to run and manage the network security solutions. The same goes for other services domains such as email and endpoint security. What are the roles and responsibilities between infrastructure teams and cyber security teams? A well-designed operating model is clear on these. Operating models should also provide guidance in terms of decision rights, accountabilities as well as clarity on owners and operators of cyber security controls. It should be noted that security cannot just be the responsibility of the cyber team. Security is everyone's responsibility and requires functional areas to take ownership and embed security considerations in their activities in alignment with the approved policies, standards, and guidelines.

Execution of a good strategy requires a high-performing cyber security team. Dedicated focus needs to be placed on attracting, retaining, and upskilling great talent in the team. Investing in people's growth and skills through continuous training is one of the more effective retention mechanisms. I recommend taking a structured approach to this through cyber skills frameworks such as the NIST National Initiative for Cyber security Education (NICE) framework. This can then help with development plans that could include certifications, courses, secondments and on-the-job training.

I am also a big advocate of keeping an open mind and demonstrating a commitment to enabling professionals from traditionally non-technology disciplines to join and contribute to cyber security. I maintain that the often talked about skills shortage in cyber security is more a shortage of imagination and a by-product of an antiquated recruitment process, including poorly worded generic job descriptions and unreasonable experience requirements. I urge you to think differently. To encourage diversity of thought. As you can glean from this book already, cyber security encompasses a lot of disciplines beyond just technical. Backgrounds including but not limited to finance, legal, marketing, risk, and audit, all have very transferable skills in the cyber security domain. We can and we must do better on this front.

A good cyber security strategy is underpinned by a well-thought-out Enterprise Security Architecture (ESA). The ESA should be aligned with the overall Enterprise Architecture and encompasses people, processes, and technologies with a focus on defence in depth. A well-designed architecture function should have an approved set of patterns for common use-cases such as remote access to business applications, use of Application Programmable Interfaces, authentication, and authorisation processes.

The ESA guides the creation of these patterns by setting the tone with principles that need to be considered. ESA also provides a representation of the current state of security capability and guides the selection of tools and technologies for domains that are required to deliver the target state architecture.

Target state architecture evolves to support cyber security strategy, and if decisions need to be made related to security controls for projects or applications, the ESA serves as a reference point for these. Decisions not aligned with target state architecture risk incurring technical debt or inefficiencies. However, sometimes, these might be necessary to support business priorities. In the absence of a reference architecture, these decisions cannot be taken in an informed manner.

The importance of evolving security architecture to respond to changing landscape cannot be overstated. For example, the rapid change in ways of working and a massive spike in remote working has necessitated a material shift in how security controls need to be designed and managed. This includes a shift away from the static network perimeter controls to nimbler identity-centric, adaptive authentication, and endpoint focussed models. Industry architectural approaches such as Zero Trust also evolve to meet the new challenges and requirements, so it is vital that an ESA is dynamic enough to accommodate them as necessary.

Good ESA should look at future proofing as well as highlighting overlaps or gaps in key cyber security capabilities, which can assist with investment and resourcing decisions. This can help address one of the common challenges faced by many organisations which is tool sprawl where there are many security solutions and technologies running in the environment that aren't optimised and lead to inefficiencies and wastage of time and resources.

Organisational culture has a far-reaching impact on security strategy and architecture. Good cyber security culture cannot exist in the absence of a good overall organisational culture, so it is incumbent upon exceptional cyber security leaders and professionals to understand and operate in harmony with it. Industries such as higher education are based on a culture of openness, sharing and collaboration. Cyber security programs in these organisations are going to look very different than those in financial services, which are typically more heavily regulated. Implementing highly prescriptive technical controls in areas such as end-user computing will likely be met with much greater resistance in higher education environments than in financial services, where it could be more acceptable.

Hopefully, this rule has given you a good overview of what it takes to build, run, and lead optimal cyber security strategies and outcomes.

"The will to win, the desire to succeed, the urge to reach your full potential, these are the keys that will unlock the door to personal excellence."

— **Confucius**

Master the Art of Differentiating Skills

What sets apart merely good professionals from exceptional professionals are generally the soft skills. Now soft skills are a widely used term that can mean different things to different people. For our purpose, we'll use the term to mean non-technical skills. I prefer to call these differentiating skills as opposed to soft skills. In my experience, these skills are the ones that make a difference between two people with similar technical prowess, but one becoming highly successful and the other remaining mediocre. These differentiating skills include but are not limited to business writing, communication, presentation, storytelling, networking, and the right mindset. I started with business writing as the first one on the list, and that's no accident. Writing is one of the most underrated but vital differentiating skill.

The art of good writing becomes critical as you move up the organisational hierarchy or become a more seasoned practitioner in the field. Good writing includes tailoring your messages for the appropriate audience – succinctly and sharply. I recommend using simple English and shorter sentences that are not convoluted. This encompasses all written communication such as emails, memos, reports, and formal papers. Writing also means being able to package discussion items in a structured manner – so there is a clear start, middle, and finish. The key here is to articulate the ask clearly and early - what is the outcome you desire of the artefact, and why are you writing it. For example, are you seeking endorsement, is it just for noting, are you seeking specific assistance, is an action required – if so, by when? Remember, most senior executives and stakeholders are time-poor and dealing with multiple, competing priorities, so you need to get to the point quickly. Prior to sending your artefacts to senior executives, I suggest bouncing it off someone trusted in the organisation but outside your security area to confirm if the message makes sense, is clear and free from jargon. I know a lot of these things may appear to be common sense but let me assure you that in my years of experience and talking to peers and other industry experts, good writing skills are hard to find. Too many professionals get stuck at a mid-career level due to a lack of strong writing skills.

On my podcast, I have the privilege to discuss various aspects of cyber security, leadership, and growth with acclaimed experts. The strong correlation between good writers and presenters is astounding. When you write and package things well, it becomes smoother and more efficient to present that information well too. This, in turn, gives the presenter more confidence leading to more areas they can authoritatively speak on. I hope I have made my thoughts on the importance of good writing skills abundantly clear.

Now, another critical skill for success that also leverages writing skills is what I call "Think in Options". During the course of your cyber security career, regardless of your seniority, you'll be in positions where you're required to solve very complex problems. This could include anything from addressing the increasing demand for cyber security services with limited resources, making a recommendation on renewal of tools or technologies, addressing organisational cyber risk, and changing investment profile. Always remember that a key role of a cyber security professional is of a strategic advisor. This is even more important in senior positions. When you think in options, you can serve as a trusted advisor. A valued advisor doesn't just give you a problem but also options to solve it with associated pros and cons. Remember, you're always speaking the business and risk language, so any options paper needs to consider these. You must include the financial and risk impact along with implementation confidence for each option. As a rule of thumb, aim to have three options but not over five. Always include a recommended option and your rationale for it. One of your options should describe what would happen if you did nothing and the pros and cons that come with it. This is important because it provides decision-makers with some context for the solutions and recommendations in your other options. It also serves as a reference point and gives them a sense of what could happen if no further actions were taken. Your audience are likely senior leaders, so keep the options free of jargon and ideally include a single table where you can see the options side-by-side.

Some practical advice – if you are proposing options related to a security tool or technology, I highly recommend you break this down into real-life use cases that help the organisation. Security tools by themselves mean nothing unless they are delivering specific outcomes. These outcomes are the use-cases from which the organisation derives value. A good way to enable appropriate use-cases is to think of control objectives for any technology that is being considered and then get specific. For example, PAM products address the control objective of managing privileged users, accounts, and their activities on critical applications. Use cases for the PAM product could include password lifecycle management and privileged session recording. There might be other functionalities that the product can offer, but you need to articulate the ones that are relevant for your purposes. It's prudent to provide a breakdown of use-cases in options as opposed to just stating the name of a tool.

The other key differentiating skill is the art of storytelling. Now, stories have a deep connection with humans through our evolution. Stories have been a critical piece in our growth as a civilisation. Great stories have been used throughout human history to pass down wisdom and frameworks to operate in our world. Great spiritual texts have relied on stories. Disciplines such as neuroscience show the importance of stories in evoking emotions and consequently inspiring actions and decisions. If you master the art of storytelling, you'll become an unstoppable force in your leadership, communication, and persuasion skills.

There are practical ways to incorporate storytelling in your presentations, such as using analogies, and images, and ensuring your artefacts or slides clearly connect to the primary purpose of the session. Challenge yourself to cut down on text as much as possible. Ask yourself – does this content really need to be there. Wordy slides are poor in getting engagement.

When doing presentations, ensure you know your audience and start with a catchy image or statistic. This will help get your audience's attention. People generally decide within the first minute how engaged they'd be with the presentation. I'd also recommend projecting your voice well when presenting. This gives the audience a sense of confidence in the speaker and will make you feel more comfortable.

I have personally used these techniques many times in my public talks and keynotes to senior executive audiences. In some cases, I have delivered presentations through slide decks that had only pictures and no text. I distinctly remembered a keynote to a group of senior cyber security and technology leaders in Australia. The tone I wanted to set through my session was ensuring people were maximising cyber security engagement in their organisations to achieve meaningful success. Now, I could have opened my presentation with some text to that effect, but that would have been expected and boring. Instead, I opened my presentation with a high-definition picture of a very scary clown. I had requested the conference organisers to keep the lighting level in the room at a low setting which further magnified the scary image. This immediately got everyone's attention and enabled me to make my point of what a cyber security function comes across to people when it isn't business-aligned, only imposes requirements, isn't pragmatic and exclusively talks about incidents and breaches. It's not something that people want to engage with. The rest of the presentation had pictures varying from emojis to posters in trains that I leveraged to talk about effective ways to drive engagement. I still have people who talk to me about the good impact of that keynote session and the distinctive style of only using images. Hopefully, this gave you some ideas on doing your own presentation a bit differently. There are many great resources on the internet about improving the story-telling skills you can leverage. I have included some in the resources section.

An attribute that makes a meaningful contribution to influencing and negotiating with stakeholders as well as being effective in your own role is honing your emotional intelligence. This skill allows you to read a room, understand what your stakeholders are thinking and be able to empathise with their point of view. This then enables you to tailor your messaging in a manner that will resonate with your audience and maximise your chances of success. Emotional intelligence requires you to manage your own emotions by being mindful and knowing what triggers them. Being a cyber security leader involves encountering some very stressful situations especially when you are dealing with a significant incident or attack. Being able to manage your state and control your emotions go a long way in helping you optimally deal with these situations.

Emotional intelligence involves a level of self-awareness where you are conscious of how you may come across to other people. It is possible to get carried away and become too attached to your security assessment reports and recommendations and expect the business to drop everything and fix what you think needs fixing. This is where the ability to control your impulses and put yourself in your stakeholder's shoes will stop you from overreacting and allow a constructive outcome grounded in empathy, pragmatism, and a shared desire to achieve what's best for your organisation. We humans are driven by emotions. Our decision making is significantly impacted if our emotions are impaired. Developing emotional intelligence allows you to make good quality decisions and serve as an effective partner to your stakeholders and business.

Now, exceptional professionals also work on keeping their energy levels high. Their enthusiasm and energy go a long way in establishing and growing stakeholder relationships. It also makes a noticeable difference when delivering presentations. My way of managing energy levels is by eating plant-based foods, ensuring I get some form of exercise every day – even if it's just a 30-minute walk, taking cold showers, and doing some breathwork. I have found these help me stay sharp and healthy. You need to find what works for you. There is a very real challenge in the cyber security industry of good people being burnt out, so I urge you to prioritise your physical and mental health and wellbeing before anything else.

One more skill vital to professional and personal success is networking. Now, networking comes inherently with certain connotations in people's minds. Some folks think of it as a forced activity requiring them to sell something. Others look at it as an opportunity to meet and greet new people and form professional connections, while a category of people do it because they have been encouraged by books, articles, or coaches to do so. To me, networking is part of a growth mindset. Growth mindset is a state where you're continuously learning and developing new skills. All in the pursuit of becoming a person of value and looking at every avenue to add value to your organisations, clients, and customers.

Networking comes in many stripes and forms. It isn't about sales or a job search. It is about connecting with communities and people who contribute to our growth while allowing us to positively affect them. Networking can include professional or industry associations. It can include conferences and volunteer groups.

It can also include informal forums such as online communities or Meetups (https://www.meetup.com).

Networking can lead to several happy coincidences. Keep an open mind and get to know other people. Ask them about their work and interests. This will allow you to hopefully learn new things while organically forming a connection. Most people are more than happy to reciprocate. So, if you show genuine interest in understanding people and their challenges, they'll do the same. This then allows you to get value out of the discussion. Whether it is knowing more about opportunities in the industry or potential areas of business or what skills you need to acquire. This all becomes possible through effective networking. And sometimes, none of these happen, and that's okay. You still improved your people skills through another interaction. There are no failures in a growth mindset. Just learning.

I have benefitted massively from networking, including being part of professional associations. For example, ISACA is a leading international industry body for cyber security, audit, and risk professionals. I have been a member of it for over a decade. Being part of the association of like-minded professionals has contributed tremendously to my own career and personal growth. A lot of my good friends today are those that I met through industry associations such as ISACA.

I'll share a quick personal story that helps show the power of networking and professional associations and how they played a key role in making my move from the United States to Australia a professional success. Now, I was an active member of the ISACA Denver Chapter for several years and knew the value and reach of the body. When I decided to move to Sydney, Australia to be closer to family, I didn't have any professional connections or leads. A logical place to start was to understand the local cyber security industry better. So naturally, I reached out to ISACA Sydney Chapter and sought assistance from them. I was lucky enough to get that time and support from the local chapter leaders. This then allowed me a much stronger platform to build and grow my career than just randomly applying for jobs online. I got assistance from the local chapter because I was part of the same international ISACA body and had focussed on organic networking to make connections within the association through regular participation in branch events. I have since been fortunate to become a Board Director with ISACA Sydney to contribute to its mission while doing my part to give back to the community.

An important attribute of any exceptional professional, but especially cyber security and technology professionals, is the adoption of a learning mindset. The world has changed dramatically just in the last couple of decades due to the technological forces of mobile devices, cloud, machine learning, and ubiquitous and relatively cheap internet access. If you weren't keeping pace with the changing technology, standards, industry, and regulatory landscape, it would be surprising if you have made material progress in your career relative to the opportunities presented.

The pace of change remains relentless. The current rise of Metaverse and Web 3.0 with Cryptocurrencies, Blockchain, Non-fungible Tokens (NFTs), and ongoing growth in the convergence of physical security and cyber security, and Internet of Things (IoTs) are just examples of this. In this world, traditional, static approaches to cyber security aren't going to cut it. A lot of elements in Web 3.0 have a decentralised structure and trust model that is fundamentally different than the one on which the traditional internet was based. This moves away from reliance on intermediaries, brokers, and hierarchical approaches to principles of distributed computing and ledgers. We need a different way of thinking and a workforce of smart cyber leaders and professionals who can adapt and successfully navigate these changing times.

My suggestion is to start with the "What" and the "Why". What exactly are these technologies, and why do they matter from a business and people benefit perspective. Starting with these questions and mindset will allow a structured approach to the identification of key assets and processes with associated threats, controls, and risks. This will require constant communication and engagement with the right stakeholders. As an example, organisations could leverage Metaverse and augmented reality to help potential customers shop and interact with their products in a far more realistic manner than is possible today. The role of trusted secure identities and user education to safeguard brand reputation and customer trust will take on a lot of importance in this endeavour which may require a change in the existing cyber security strategy and underlying toolsets related to it.

Furthermore, we're seeing increases in the adoption of Machine Learning by organisations to automate manual tasks, create operational efficiencies and offer better customer service through chatbots. For these business benefits to be realised, cyber security approaches need to incorporate protection against data poisoning and adversarial inputs. These are crucial to protecting the integrity and confidentiality of the information learnt and communicated by applications such as chatbots.

Now, you can only contribute effectively to the scenarios such as the ones above if you have been engaging with your business to understand the use cases and drivers for the adoption of new technologies. Thus, requiring you to stay updated with the latest developments and emerging trends.

Fortunately, it has never been easier to learn new skills and stay updated with all the changes. There is a plethora of podcasts, videos, free or inexpensive online courses, and reading material readily available. I have included helpful learning resources in the resources section. Additionally, building good relationships with current and potential vendors can also serve as a valuable mechanism to grow your own skills and further your understanding of the innovations in the marketplace. All it takes to feed your learning mindset is the willingness and commitment to keep improving every day. Become a better version of yourself today than you were yesterday. Tomorrow, become better than you are today. That's what it is really about. It isn't a competition with anyone else. Just between yourself tomorrow, today, and yesterday.

We have looked at a range of differentiating skills in this rule. I'll conclude with a skill that is intrinsic to a lot of areas and without which, massive success is hard to achieve. This is the skill and attribute of being able to make decisions and take action. I have seen a lot of intelligent people fall prey to paralysis by analysis. Often analysis is just an excuse for procrastination. By all means, do your research but then take decisions and act. Don't get stuck in the endless pit of reading and pondering without producing anything tangible that offers value. A good way to achieve this by setting deadlines for yourself to gather relevant information and after which you must move to the next phase of acting and delivering outcomes. Take an iterative approach where you start producing artefacts that can be progressively enhanced through consultation and feedback. Giving your stakeholders, customers, or audience something tangible to react to works so much better than just discussing high-level abstract theories.

Great ideas and knowledge serve little purpose if they are not put into action so commit yourself to becoming a person of action. This is the best way to add value. Look at any failures that come along the way as learning opportunities. Anyone who has done anything meaningful has had to endure some form of failure. That's just the process of becoming better. Doing something is the best way to learn.

Decision-making will allow you to develop an entrepreneurial mindset where you will actively find ways to solve complex problems and take advantage of opportunities presented. This will make you invaluable to your organisation and the marketplace. Essentially, you are on the path to becoming truly exceptional.

"If people like you they'll listen to you, but if they trust you, they'll do business with you."

— **Zig Ziglar**

Build an Authentic Brand

To be an exceptional cyber security leader, you need to be able to inspire confidence and influence key stakeholders. The prior rules in the book covered several elements that enable you to do this. However, it is worth acknowledging that ultimately people do business with people they trust. This is a well-accepted fact that has stood the test of time. Trust comes down to doing what you say and saying what you do. It comes through a reputation of reliability, integrity, and authenticity. However, it is awfully hard to trust people you don't know. To gain that trust, it is important to be visible, engaging, and actively help people.

Both visibility and trust become possible when you are an authentic brand by yourself, something that can work both internally in your organisation and externally. This also provides you with invaluable social proof. When you have a respected brand, and you show up to a meeting, put forward a proposal or do a presentation, there is already inherent credibility established, and this makes achieving your objectives so much easier. This can also serendipitously open doors for you to make amazing strides in your career journey.

Building a brand requires professionals to be comfortable in making their voices heard. This involves a degree of promotion. Now, promotion sometimes gets a bad name amongst cyber security and technology professionals. However, I believe that promotion, including self-promotion, is only bad if you have nothing valuable to offer or you don't believe in what you're saying. If you have something valuable to offer - some unique insight or something that others can find useful, you owe it to yourself, your organisation, and the industry to speak out and share that knowledge. We are living in an age where we are overloaded with information. What we need is not more information but clarity and wisdom. Wisdom that comes from unique perspectives and lived experiences.

Unfortunately, I have observed that many wise professionals who are really good at cyber security are often not comfortable or willing to present and share their experiences, even within their own organisations! We need these people to be more vocal and active to enable value delivery through cyber security. They must work hard to overcome impostor syndrome and other hesitations and build confidence to share their skills and knowledge more widely. If you are one of the professionals who is still on the fence when it comes to sharing your insights, I encourage you to be brave and take massive action immediately. Being brave doesn't mean you aren't scared; it means you do something despite the fear.

I acknowledge that this can be difficult for people so let us look at some practical ways to make this happen. The easiest starting point is to share thoughts on something you are currently working on or have recently completed. This could involve a project, technical implementation, or a certification. You can share your thoughts on how you approached it and the associated learnings. Obviously, be smart about ensuring appropriate confidentiality of the initiative. You can use any medium that you are comfortable with – written post, video, presentation or just a verbal update to your team.

A smart approach is leveraging the power of social media. However, please do not be lazy in doing this. If you are sharing an external article that you read, take some time to write a few lines on your key takeaways. The same applies if you recently attended a conference or completed a course. Do not just post that you did these, rather, share the two or three things you found insightful. This will get you engagement and position yourself as somebody actively contributing to the industry. In the initial stages of using professional social media platforms, it is prudent to avoid a scatter-gun approach of sharing anything and everything under the sun. Rather, make a concerted effort to focus on a handful of topics. Depending on your interest, these could be – security tools, cloud adoption, emerging technologies, regulatory changes, career growth, governance, risk management, culture, and training. Whatever areas you pick, stay focussed on them for at least 3 to 4 months. This will help you channel your energies better and build more confidence in the subject areas. Don't get discouraged if your initial posts don't get as much engagement as you'd like. The important thing here is to be consistent and persistent. As you continue to post more valuable content, the likelihood of some of it becoming popular increases.

One of the most effective mechanisms to add value with your knowledge is to adopt a curiosity mindset. This will help you ask good questions and challenge the status quo. These questions and your desire to get them answered will serve you really well in your journey of sharing content, getting engagement, and establishing a brand.

To bolster your engagement further, it is paramount that you keep adding more people to your network. Again, the idea is not to be haphazard about it. Connect with people whose job titles and disciplines are related to the topics you have chosen to focus on. In the beginning stages of branding, depth is a more valuable ally than breadth.

You should also connect with people who you think are doing well in terms of sharing useful content. Message them with your appreciation and offer your assistance in helping them cascade their tips. Being associated with good brands increases your own brand proposition. In my experience, most people who have achieved success are only happy to give back. I am happy for you to contact me via LinkedIn, my website, or other channels. I'll do my best to help you on the journey of promoting valuable content.

Some more ideas to get started with growing and sharing your expertise:

- Join and contribute to professional associations and industry-specific groups such as ISACA, Australian Information Security Association (AISA), ISC2, Financial Services Information Sharing and Analysis Center (FS-ISAC), Cloud Security Alliance, etc. You can contribute in several ways, such as presenting at chapter meetings or events, writing articles, and volunteering.

- Social media channels such as LinkedIn. Make social media work for you as opposed to just letting it consume you!

- Start your own blog post.

- Sharing through websites such as Medium (https://medium.com/)

- Presenting at your local industry events.

- Submitting your topic to Call for Papers for conferences you are interested in attending.

- Presenting at your organisations' All Team meetings.

- Sharing on your organisation's internal communication channels.

As you share your insights and build a brand, remember that the most important attribute for your success will be a helping mindset with an objective to serve others and provide value to them. I like aligning with the principles of educating, entertaining, and inspiring when it comes to sharing content. Ensure that you maintain integrity in your interactions so people can trust you. I will also add adaptability and authenticity to the list. Adaptability is where you are constantly sharing content that is relevant to the times. Authenticity is where you present your true self. Be who you are. Not anyone else. There is a lot of power to being authentic in a world increasingly focused on presenting a fake, overly choreographed shiny facade.

As you build your authentic personal brand, you can apply the same principles to do it for your team as well. Guide the team to actively add value to your customers and stakeholders. Get your team to celebrate and promote wins while highlighting their excellent work across the organisation. Most organisations have internal collaboration channels and forums that can be leveraged for this purpose. A powerful team brand along with a credible personal brand will put you in a very advantageous position.

You can leverage well-known marketing models such as AIDA to assist in your brand-building exercise. AIDA stands for

Awareness, Interest, Desire, and Action. You can apply this in a cyber security context by ensuring as many people as possible know about the services you offer and communicate them in a way that makes it relatable to different audiences. This will create awareness and interest. The desire to work with you and take your advice will come when you demonstrate a pragmatic, business-aligned mindset and tangibly show how adopting secure practices and solutions will enable your customers and stakeholders to meet their objectives and aspirations in a way that safeguards trust, builds confidence, and delivers outcomes. Finally, you need to make it as easy and intuitive as possible for your audience to action your recommendations.

While enhancing your brand, I encourage you to think strategically about your career and not chase titles. Identify what you are good at and where you can be the most effective. Don't think that moving up the corporate ladder and managing large teams is the only way to achieve success. People have carved out remarkably successful careers as individual contributors in capacities such as technologists, strategists, or by working cross-functionally to drive major programs of work. Do not let conventional wisdom dictate your career path.

Now, one of the problems with the world today is that fools are too certain while intelligent people are full of self-doubt. Let us look at the cyber security field. There is massive attention to this topic as we have discussed in this book. While this presents great opportunities for current and aspiring cyber security professionals to make a difference, it also comes with a lot of responsibility and requires integrity. I am all for people looking to make more money, but it should be done through delivering value, not through selling fear, buzzwords, and doubt in the name of cyber security as we are frequently witnessing in the industry. Everyone wants a slice of the cyber security market, which is leading to questionable practices from some vendors and individuals. This is where it is important that smart people who actually know their stuff become more assertive and visible. These people can cut through the hype and uncertainty and give confidence to those that rely on cyber security professionals to do their jobs well. They can also ensure that investments are made wisely, and human aspirations are promoted.

By being strategic in your approach and building an authentic brand, you are setting yourself apart from mediocrity. You are making a difference, future-proofing your career, and on a path to being exceptional!

> *"Intellectual growth should commence at birth and cease only at death."*

> — **Albert Einstein**

Coda

The focus of this book has been to provide practical, actionable, real-world takeaways. Often a question is asked or expected of cyber security leaders on what their first 90-100 days would look like from a strategic perspective. Following the rules in the book should help you formulate this. It all starts with understanding the organisation's business and technology drivers and then connecting the cyber security vision to enable them. I have provided a high-level overview of what your first 90 days in security leadership should look like to succeed in your role. To be successful as a cyber leader, I strongly urge you to listen, observe and build relationships first as opposed to jumping straight into delivery mode.

90-day Plan Phases typically include Prepare and Evaluate, Plan and Execute, Measure and Adapt.

Prepare and Evaluate (0-45 days)

- Develop an understanding of the organisation's business, including key products and services.

- Become familiar with the mission, vision, and values of the organisation, along with its structure and lines of business.

- Gain visibility into the main priorities for the organisation, including large programs and projects in-flight and planned. Make sure you understand the benefits that these programs and projects have committed to delivering as well as their current status.

- Identify, and meet with key stakeholders to align on expectations from cyber security, including what's working, pain points and opportunities.

- Set foundations for developing meaningful relationships with your team and stakeholders through listening and engagement sessions.

- Understand current resourcing related to the team in terms of capacity and financials.

- Review material documentation, including policies, architectural artefacts, and recent audits and assessments.

- Understand the critical assets and the criteria (classification, categorisation, etc.) that inform them.

- Gauge the current cyber control maturity across major domains – governance, operational and technical. These could include access management, vulnerability management, threat and risk management, security architecture, governance, awareness, and incident preparedness. Focus on how these relate to the high-level cyber threats, audits, or risk findings. You do not need to deep dive just yet. It is more about getting a sense of the domains that require your attention over the coming weeks.

- Understand expectations around the target state maturity based on discussions with executives and key stakeholders across business and technology.

Plan and Execute (35-80 days)

- Prioritise 3-5 outcomes that deliver maximum value to the organisation.

- Prepare a high-level view of activities, milestones, and resources required to achieve the desired state.

- Through socialisation and iteration, formalise the plan and objectives and execute on quick wins.

- Establish a strong working relationship and cadence with key stakeholders.

- Get actively involved with key programs, projects, and governance forums.

Measure and Adapt (60-90 days)

- Evidence of early progress and achievements through reporting, stakeholder feedback, and metrics.

- An initial status report for leadership teams outlining observations and recommendations.

- Adapt the approach based on measurements and feedback.

Now, let us quickly summarise the 7 rules we covered in the book.

- **Rule 1** emphasised the importance of developing a business-aligned mindset to the success of cyber security professionals and programs. It covered the resources and avenues needed for this business-focussed approach. The rule discussed the importance of financial literacy and included practical tips on what cyber security leaders should know to optimise their current and future services. The rule also addressed the crucial area of getting senior leadership and executive support.

- **Rule 2** explored how cyber security is essentially a risk management exercise. Through examples, the rule explained and illustrated how cyber threats, vulnerabilities, risks, and controls come together to frame a holistic understanding of the security posture of the organisation. A major area covered was quantifying cyber security risks as far as possible. The need and ways for close alignment of cyber risks with the organisational enterprise risk framework, processes and taxonomy was also conveyed.

- **Rule 3** explained why measuring and benchmarking the progress and control posture of cyber security programs and activities is paramount. The rule covered what good metrics and measurements look like and how they can be formulated through alignment with strategic organisational assets and priorities. There were several practical steps outlined related to leveraging control frameworks and maturity levels.

- **Rule 4** established how cyber security is fundamentally a human issue. The rule covered actionable advice regarding embedding a positive security culture in the organisation through effective stakeholder management and communication of cyber security services and objectives. The necessity and ideas to evolve cyber security awareness from a boring, one-off activity to a dynamic, role-based, just-in-time construct that engages people and helps embed secure practices in their daily activities were highlighted.

- **Rule 5** provided a practical and holistic approach for building and executing cyber security strategies that enables organisational strategies and objectives. The discussion areas included the vital elements that go into designing the strategy, such as business and technology drivers, regulations, risk, and threat landscape. The importance of sourcing strategies, operating models, fit-for-purpose enterprise security architecture, organisational culture, and a high-performing team to the successful execution of the strategy was covered.

- **Rule 6** looked at the differentiating skills that contribute to professional excellence and upwards career mobility. These included writing, communication, storytelling, and networking skills, among other valuable insights, such as fostering a growth and learning mindset.

- **Rule 7** highlighted the importance of a personal and professional brand to build credibility, influence key decision-makers, and achieve desired outcomes. The rule also explained the need for knowledgeable professionals to become more visible and share their message widely through building a brand grounded in authenticity, integrity, and a desire to educate and help. There were several resources and ideas presented to aid with branding.

In conclusion, I would like to express my deep gratitude to you for reading this book and investing in your own career growth. I hope this book has given you actionable steps to further the noble mission of cyber security. If you found this book useful, my humble request is for you to share the word with at least five more people so this important message can cascade further, and we can enable more exceptional cyber security leaders and professionals. I also sincerely hope this is not the end of our conversation and request you to connect with me on LinkedIn or through my website ChiragDJoshi.com.

I also encourage you to check out my podcast, where my whole focus is on growth and learning mindset and differentiating skills in cyber security. I have been fortunate to have renowned experts join me in these conversations to share tangible insights.

I am always striving to improve the quality of my work, so any feedback that you would like to share with me is very welcome! I'd love to hear your stories and experiences of utilising the rules laid out in the book in your own careers.

References and Resources

References

Chowdhury, R., Sharot, T., Wolfe, T., Düzel, E., & Dolan, R. J. (2014). Optimistic update bias increases in older age. Psychological medicine, 44(9), 2003–2012. doi:10.1017/S0033291713002602

Moutsiana, C., Garrett, N., Clarke, R. C., Lotto, R. B., Blakemore, S. J., & Sharot, T. (2013). Human development of the ability to learn from bad news. Proceedings of the National Academy of Sciences of the United States of America, 110(41), 16396–16401. doi:10.1073/pnas.1305631110

TEDx Talks. 2014. "How to motivate yourself to change your behavior | Tali Sharot | TEDxCambridge." YouTube video,

16:48. Posted October 28, 2014. https://www.youtube.com/watch?v=xp0O2vi8DX4

Resources

Please visit ChiragDJoshi.com for the latest version of these resources.

Colonial Pipeline Incident

- https://www.bloomberg.com/news/articles/2021-06-04/hackers-breached-colonial-pipeline-using-compromised-password
- https://www.techtarget.com/whatis/feature/Colonial-Pipeline-hack-explained-Everything-you-need-to-know

Ransomware impacting Healthcare

- https://ia.acs.org.au/article/2021/victorian-hospitals-hit-by-cyber-attack.html
- https://www.itnews.com.au/news/unitingcare-queensland-hit-by-cyber-attack-563812
- https://www.infosecurity-magazine.com/news/ireland-healthcare-it-offline/

- https://www.wired.com/story/ransomware-hospitals-ryuk-trickbot/

Ransomware impacting Costa Rica:

- https://www.theguardian.com/world/2022/may/12/costa-rica-national-emergency-ransomware-attacks
- https://www.abc.net.au/news/science/2022-06-04/costa-rica-at-war-with-russian-hackers-cyber-criminals/101116930

SolarWinds breach

https://www.businessinsider.com/solarwinds-hack-explained-government-agencies-cyber-security-2020-12

Kaseya breach

https://www.zdnet.com/article/updated-kaseya-ransomware-attack-faq-what-we-know-now/

Cyber Risk and Controls

- NIST Risk Management Framework: https://csrc.nist.gov/projects/risk-management/about-rmf
- NIST Cyber Security Framework: https://www.nist.gov/cyberframework

- ISO 27001: https://www.iso.org/isoiec-27001-information-security.html

- PCI DSS: https://www.pcisecuritystandards.org/pci_security/

- FAIR: https://www.fairinstitute.org/

- Center for Internet Security Critical Security Controls: https://www.cisecurity.org/controls/cis-controls-list

- Australian Cyber Security Centre Essential 8: https://www.cyber.gov.au/acsc/view-all-content/essential-eight

Cyber Threat Modelling

- MITRE: https://attack.mitre.org/
- STRIDE: https://docs.microsoft.com/en-us/azure/security/develop/threat-modeling-tool-threats
- OWASP: https://owasp.org/www-community/Threat_Modeling_Process

- Cyber Security for Small and Medium-sized Businesses

- https://www.cyber.gov.au/acsc/small-and-medium-businesses

- https://staysafeonline.org/resources/cybersecurity-for-business/

- https://www.ncsc.gov.uk/section/information-for/small-medium-sized-organisations

Examples of Security Ratings Solutions

- Security Scorecard: https://securityscorecard.com/
- BitSight: https://www.bitsight.com/third-party-risk-management

- UpGuard: https://www.upguard.com

Cyber Security Tabletop Exercise Scenarios

- https://www.cisa.gov/cisa-tabletop-exercises-packages
- https://www.cisecurity.org/insights/white-papers/six-tabletop-exercises-prepare-cybersecurity-team

Enterprise Security Architecture

- NIST Zero Trust Architecture: https://csrc.nist.gov/publications/detail/sp/800-207/final

- SABSA: https://sabsa.org/sabsa-executive-summary/

- The Open Group Architecture Framework (TOGAF): https://pubs.opengroup.org/architecture/togaf9-doc/arch/

Cyber Security Reports

- https://www.verizon.com/business/resources/reports/dbir/

- https://www.proofpoint.com/au/resources/threat-reports/human-factor

- https://www.ic3.gov/Home/AnnualReports

Cyber Security Storytelling Resources

- https://theanalogiesproject.org/

- https://youtu.be/uIF0zZA-rYk

Websites for Cyber Security News, Information and Learning

- https://www.krebsonsecurity.com

- https://www.theregister.co.uk/security/

- https://mysecuritymarketplace.com/

- https://ismg.io/

- https://www.youtube.com/user/MySecurityAustralia

APRA CPS 234

https://www.apra.gov.au/sites/default/files/cps_234_july_2019_for_public_release.pdf

Australian Energy Sector Cyber Security Framework

https://aemo.com.au/initiatives/major-programs/cyber-security/aescsf-framework-and-resources

GDPR

https://gdpr.eu/

NIST NICE Skills Framework

https://csrc.nist.gov/publications/detail/sp/800-181/rev-1/final

Cloud Computing

- AWS: https://aws.amazon.com

- Microsoft Azure: https://azure.microsoft.com/

- Google Cloud: https://cloud.google.com/

Professional Associations and Industry Groups

- ISACA: https://www.isaca.org/

- AISA: https://www.aisa.org.au

- ISC2: https://www.isc2.org/

- OWASP: https://www.owasp.org

- Cloud Security Alliance: https://cloudsecurityalliance.org/

- FS-ISAC: https://www.fsisac.com/

Information on Deep Fakes and Scams using Artificial Intelligence

- https://www.theguardian.com/technology/2020/jan/13/what-are-deepfakes-and-how-can-you-spot-them

- https://www.wsj.com/articles/fraudsters-use-ai-to-mimic-ceos-voice-in-unusual-cybercrime-case-11567157402

- https://spectrum.ieee.org/tech-talk/artificial-intelligence/machine-learning/will-deepfakes-detection-be-ready-for-2020

Information on Data Poisoning and Adversarial Inputs

- https://www.theguardian.com/technology/2016/mar/26/microsoft-deeply-sorry-for-offensive-tweets-by-ai-chatbot
- https://skylightcyber.com/2019/07/18/cylance-i-kill-you/

AIDA Model

https://www.oxfordreference.com/view/10.1093/oi/authority.20110803095432783

Chirag's Best-Selling Book – 7 Rules to Influence Behaviour and Win at Cyber Security Awareness:

- Amazon: https://www.amazon.com.au/dp/B07VPP71BN
- E-books: https://books2read.com/Cybersecurityawareness

Chirag's Podcast

- YouTube: https://www.youtube.com/channel/UCnbyecINaNr13VgXfN8eEtg

- Spotify: https://open.spotify.com/show/5HRYS0aKyDh5SumJbfB4m5

- Anchor: https://anchor.fm/chirag-joshi0

About the Author

Chirag's ambitious goal is simple—to enable human progress through trust in technology. To accomplish this, he wants to help build a world where there is trust in digital systems, protection against cyber threats, and a safe environment online for communication, commerce, and engagement. He is especially passionate about the safety of children and vulnerable sections of society online. This goal has served as a motivation that has led Chirag to become a sought-after speaker and advocate at various industry-leading conferences and events. Chirag is respected as a thought leader in cyber security with keynotes and presentations at forums in the United States, Australia, and Asia. His podcast features insights from distinguished professionals in a wide range of disciplines, including media, entrepreneurship, executive leadership, and futurology.

He is the author of the highly successful book "7 Rules to Influence Behaviour and Win at Cyber Security Awareness" which has been purchased in over 11 countries across the world and became an Amazon Australia Best-Seller in its category.

During the course of his career spanning multiple sectors and countries, he has built, implemented, and successfully managed cyber security, risk management, compliance, and awareness programs. The success of these programs was a result of unyielding focus on business priorities, a pragmatic approach to cyber threats, and, most importantly, effective stakeholder engagement. Chirag has held senior leadership positions in large, complex organisations and excels at the art of translating business and technical speak in a manner that optimises value.

Chirag has also conducted several successful cyber security education sessions for executives and non-technical audiences in diverse industries such as finance, energy, healthcare, and higher education. He has led teams, managed multi-million-dollar budget and transformation programs. He has experience in both IT and OT environments, and leading cyber security through de-mergers and divestments.

Chirag has extensive experience with a wide range of standards, frameworks, and regulations, including NIST CSF, APRA CPS 234, AESCSF, PCI DSS, Health Insurance Portability and Accountability Act (HIPAA) and ISO 27001/2.

Chirag's academic qualifications include a master's degree in telecommunications management from Oklahoma State University and a bachelor's degree in electronics and telecommunications engineering from the University of Mumbai. He holds multiple certifications, including Certified Information Security Manager, Certified Information Systems Auditor, Certified in Risk and Information Systems Control, and Certified Data Privacy Solutions Engineer.

His areas of expertise include strategic cyber advisory to executives, cyber risk management, cyber strategy and architecture, security and technology governance, cyber transformation programs and security awareness training.